CREATIVE IS A VERB

PATTI DIGH

IF You'RE alive, You'RE Creative

TWITTER SUMMARY: STOP MEASURING
YOUR CREATIVITY. YOUR LIFE
IS THE WORK OF ART.

skirt!

Guilford , Connecticut
An imprint of Globe Pequot Press

skirt!® is an imprint of Globe Pequot Press.

skirt!® is a registered trademark of Morris Book Publishing Group, LLC, and is used with express permission.

Design by Diana Nuhn

Library of Congress Cataloging-in-Publication Data is available on file.

ISBN 978-1-59921-883-0

Printed in the United States of America

10 9 8 7 6 5 4 3 2 1

Creativity is piercing the mundane to find the marvelous. —**Bill Moyers**

This book is

for everyone who courageously creates their life as a work of art,
sometimes beautiful, sometimes messy, sometimes painful,
sometimes mundane, and always an expression of their unique vision;

for everyone who notices the color chartreuse and crazy clouds
wherever they go;

for everyone who makes art from stones, from trash, from loss;

for everyone who longs to climb back into the marvelous;

for everyone who yearns to reclaim their creative spirit,
their art spark; and

for those who want to jump into their yearning
and walk toward their obstacles.

Yes, I mean you.

for Celeste Rast, whose life was a
fantastic creative spark.

and for John, Emma, and Tessie because.

just because. everything.

Contents

When I say be creative,
I don't mean
you should all go
and become great painters
and great poets.

I simply mean
let your life
be a painting,
let your life
be a poem.

—Osho

Introduction

IF YOU'RE ALIVE, YOU'RE CREATIVE

Love the art in yourself, not yourself in the art. —**Konstantin Stanislavsky**

We sat deep into the night, talking. The rugged red mesas of Jemez Springs, New Mexico, surrounded us. The landscape and spaciousness had inspired great cooking and long talks in front of the fire.

A few years ago my business and creative partner, David Robinson, and I carved out a week to sit and talk and think about what we wanted to create together in the world. Friends had opened their home to us, leaving us alone in an exquisite, Japanese-inspired space.

If you're alive, you're creative . . . we "reduce" and "deflect" our creative selves in many ways. Life is the creative acti not the canvas or the blank page.

And so we sat. The talk turned to art. Our urge was to create workshops and retreats and corporate trainings that were artful. We wanted to create symphony projects that would string together original music, art, and narrative to tell stories we believed needed to be told. We longed to have art be at the center of all we do. But something was stopping us from doing it.

The talk turned to identity, because art—after all (and above all)—serves an identity function: Who are we? Who are we in relationship to others? What do we yearn to bring into the world? We talked about being starving artists, driven to creating what we longed to say—me in words, and David in paint—and finally I asked David a question that made him sit looking at me, speechless. It was a question that also surprised me:

"David," I said, "if you really believed your art could truly provide everything you ever wanted or needed in your life, how would that change the way you approach it?"

YOU CAN BE CREATIVE ONLY IF YOU LOVE LIFE ENOUGH THAT YOU WANT TO ENHANCE ITS BEAUTY.

—Osho

We sat in silence a long time, each pondering that question. And then we talked about how that belief would free us up to put creating at the center.

David then turned to me. "Patti," he said, "why is it that when someone asks you what you do, you never say you're a writer?"

I laughed (my deflection of choice, of habit). "Because I'm not a writer, David, not really. I'm not a real writer, not like Richard Powers or Anne Lamott or Herman Melville or . . ."

> NOTHING FEEDS THE CENTER OF BEING SO MUCH AS CREATIVE WORK.
>
> —Anne Morrow Lindbergh

He looked at me and smiled a quiet smile. "What bar have you set for yourself, Patti?" he asked. "You've written three books and published over a hundred articles. What exactly would make you a writer?"

The next day we went into Santa Fe for lunch with an acquaintance, a man we had met but didn't know well. Robin turned to me at the beginning of the meal. "Patti, what do you do?"

I looked over the table at David, who was waiting expectantly for my answer. I smiled and said, "I'm a writer." All puffed up and proud for showing David I could do it, I was unprepared for Robin's next question.

"Really," he said. "What do you write?"

"Oh, nothing, really. I just write these little essays every Monday."

David nodded his head ever so slightly and looked down, with a tiny smile. Afterward, he turned to me as we walked back to our car. "Oh, nothing, really? You just write these little essays every Monday?"

We minimize ourselves in so many ways, and stop ourselves from living our most creative life—or owning that we are creative beings *just because we are alive.* Often without realizing it.

> The longing to produce great inspirations didn't produce anything but more longing.
>
> —**Sophie Kerr**

We deflect and reduce with laughter, with language, with *little.* We learn—sometimes in childhood and certainly later—to diminish the bright light we bring into the world, to make it smaller, to hide it, put a shade on it. We do it for many reasons: to raise others up, to avoid comparisons, to minimize the fall when we fail, to protect and explain and rationalize and, it seems, to cover.

We don't come into the world that way. "Are you a writer?" I heard John ask our youngest daughter Tess before dinner tonight, having read the draft of this essay. Unlike her more measured college-bound sister, Emma, Tess responded in her first-grade voice: "YES! I'M A WRITER! I WROTE TWO BIG BOOKS!" she screamed, handing him two folded pieces of paper with drawings and letters on them.

Picasso once said, "Every child is an artist. The problem is how to remain an artist once we grow up." We're good at reducing. **What are our strategies for enlarging, expanding, growing into, being big in the world? I wonder.**

This book is about fully owning our innate creative spirit again. Not necessarily to call ourselves artists or writers, but to see our lives as creative. Not necessarily to make a living as an artist or writer, but to free ourselves up to say what we most long to say, to paint what we alone see in this vast incredible world, to build artful and joyous relationships, to leave a legacy of color and form and laughter in our wake.

We have that art spark when we are children; we lose it as we grow into the world of comparisons, perfectionism, categories like "best seller," realities of making a living, pressing tofu for dinner, changing diapers, figuring out how to put together a chest of drawers from IKEA, paying taxes, doing the same underwear in the laundry *repeatedly*.

> THE ARTIST IS NOT A SPECIAL KIND OF PERSON; RATHER EACH PERSON IS A SPECIAL KIND OF ARTIST.
>
> —**Ananda Coomaraswamy**

What would happen if we fully owned that we are creative beings, whether or not we will ever call ourselves writers or artists? Whether or not we ever pick up a quill pen or brush or camera? Whether or not we ever show anyone our art, sell any of it, or create something fantastically unique? What if we owned that making dinner was a fully creative act?

Open up.

See more.

Live deeper.

That's what art is. That's what creativity is. That's what life is.

Diderot has said, "There is no such thing as creativity." I balked when I first read that. Now I believe it's true. There's only living. And living fully, openly, deeply is a creative act. It is the original creative act.

PART ONE
Art Fear

Don't apologize for who you are

or the art you create.

—*C. J. Rider*

don't forget to write

while you are piecing together the map of your life,
stepping as nimbly as you can out of the mulch
of your thoughts, the busy traffic of your heart,
while you attempt grace and magic and the blessing of
your soft, surrendered kiss, while you are fathoming the stretch
you will need for the wide and rocky jungle of your own happiness,
while you are hunkering down to a piece of dark bread
and the odd, welcome relief of hunger,
don't forget to write.

write this day, its too-early morning and the birdsong
you cursed into your pillow. write the way the dog
looked at you as forlornly as your own shadow.
write this blanket, this cup of coffee, the irreverent

clatter of the neighbor's lawnmower. write the bees
that bend forever to their task. write the July heat
and the laps in the town pool that cleave you from
this earth, the over-solid grip you have on everything.
write this hour, tired and awake all at once, the distractions
you can make of breakfast or a calculator or the remote control
lying flaccid on the living room couch.

write the dead mosquito on the bathroom floor, the small
clot of blood on your forearm. write the careful arrangement
of the bed linens, the yellow of the walls, the way the
garden hose snakes around the back porch where old boxes
are bending under their own weight and where spiders
have begun to take control of the tomato plants.
write your white legs and your short pants and
the constellations imprinted on your skin. write
the dusty sex toys in the bedside bureau, the silvery
condom packages nearing their expiration dates.
write the wet sound of love in the middle of the night.

write the blackberry bush and its sour fruit,
the mailman in his cheerful hat,
the neighbor who confuses you with someone else,
calls you a name that's not yours, write the feeling
of lost identity and disappointment and some letter
you're perennially hoping for.

write the words for failure. write the words for hope.
write the tightrope dangling above the canyon,
and down below, the electric water furious and free.

write green. write violet. write blazing orange.
write the smell of grapefruit skin, the eyelash
on a cheekbone, the hand you hold in the dark.
write the first, honest paragraphs of sunrise.
write everything, or nothing, but don't forget to write.

—Maya Stein

CHAPTER ONE

Reclaim the Spark: Who This Book Is For

Life is pure adventure, and the sooner we realize that, the sooner we will be able to treat life as art. —**Maya Angelou**

One bright spring day when I was forty-four years old, over a sturdy cup of hot black coffee and a bowl of McCann's slow-cooking, steel-cut Irish oatmeal topped with raspberries, I realized that I couldn't tackle fear until I first got over my fear of being fearful.

Yes, that's it—I needed to let go of the fear of fearfulness before I could tackle the bigger problem of fear itself. Fear itself, it turns out, is a gift and not a burden, since it tells us important things—things we actually need to know, not like the square root of pi or the conjugation of verbs, which we can always count on our friend Rosemary to tell us, but things about ourselves—those deep real selves, the ones that don't show up on business cards, that one, there, the little one, the one we are left with when we are lying in bed looking at the ceiling. The still one. The one whose shadow looms large.

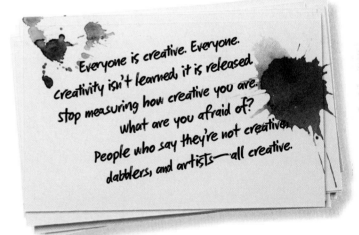

Everyone is creative. Everyone. creativity isn't learned, it is released. stop measuring how creative you are. what are you afraid of? People who say they're not creative, dabblers, and artists—all creative.

"I'm afraid of bees," my then-thirteen-year-old daughter answered when I asked about her fears. "And you—well, you're afraid of birds, bats, being buried alive," she informed me, reminding me of her concept of erasable fears—she confused "irrational fears" and called them "erasable fears" once as a child. Perfect.

Yes, I thought to myself, and not only being buried alive, but also being buried dead or in any shape or form, being found out, being forgotten, being laughed at. "Isn't fear all mental?" she continued. "Yes, I'd have to say it is," I replied.

"And **by knowing what we fear, don't we know what we care about, how we are measuring our worth, what success looks like?**" I asked. So isn't fear helpful, then?

I was in an ethics seminar once, a session bringing together adults and high school students for a dialogue. Our facilitator asked us to read "Buddhist Economics" by E. F. Schumacher from his book *Small Is Beautiful.* A high school junior woke me up with her assessment of a complex situation, with that succinct honesty only the young are good at: "When my parents divorced, my father had more money than my mother, and they were always scared and angry. He was scared he would lose his money and she was angry that he had more than her."

Not knowing is what makes us scared; being scared is what makes us angry. As Melville wrote, ignorance is the parent of fear. What if I fail as a writer, a poet, a mother, a painter? Who will love me then? How is this going to affect the rest of my life? What if they don't like what I write? I don't know them, they're different from me, I'm afraid.

I'm angry that they can't understand me; I'm scared that they might.

> WE INVENT WHAT WE LOVE AND WHAT WE FEAR.
>
> —John Irving

The brilliant book *Art and Fear* is my go-to book on the fear of creation.

Go.

Read it.

Now.

I'll wait right here.

In it David Bayles and Ted Orland write: "Fears about artmaking fall into two families: fears about yourself, and fears about your reception by others. In a general way, **fears about yourself prevent you from doing your best work, while fears about your reception by others prevent you from doing your own work.**" As Claude Bristol has written, "To live a creative life, we must lose our fear of being wrong."

We fear we can't measure up to the work of others.

We fear we can't measure up to our Selves.

We fear we can't measure up to the expectations of an audience.

And, I might add, we fear being fearful.

T. S. Eliot wrote in "The Waste Land":

> *And I will show you something different from either*
>
> *Your shadow at morning striding behind you*
>
> *Or your shadow at evening rising to meet you;*
>
> *I will show you fear in a handful of dust.*

Dust, just dust, our shadow dust. Is no one following us but ourselves? Indeed. Embrace fear and listen to its messages—it is a part of you like your shadow is. When we know what we most fear, we know what we care most about, don't we? So love fear, don't fear it.

[
The death of fear is in doing what you fear to do.
—Sequichie Comingdeer
]

Who this book is for

Children don't need this book. Not like you and I do.

The question of how to be creative—or how to be more creative—would never occur to a child, would it? No.

The very idea that there are actually words for their way of being in the world—*flat-out* and *fantastic* and *curious about everything*—would likely puzzle them. They're not being creative, they're just being fully human. Like we all are until we start getting messages about coloring inside the lines, that the sun is always yellow, that trees aren't purple, that we need to sit and be quiet, and that we can't wear white shoes before Easter or after Labor Day.

> NOW THAT YOU HAVE BROKEN THROUGH THE WALL WITH YOUR HEAD, WHAT WILL YOU DO IN THE NEIGHBORING CELL?
>
> —S. J. Lec

On my forty-city grassroots book tour for *Life Is a Verb,* I was invited to Madison, Wisconsin, by an amazing woman named Jodi Cohen. As part of my stay there, I went with Jodi on a Friday afternoon to a Jewish senior citizens' center where she played guitar and led the seniors in song. The urge toward deep ritual moved me.

"We are in the ten days of awe in the Jewish high holidays," the speaker said. "And in the ten days of awe, we remember that the first time we see something extraordinary, we call it a miracle, but when we see it over and over and over again, we just call it ordinary."

We just call it ordinary.

We have to reclaim the extraordinary in the everyday. That's where the art is.

Easier said than done, my friend.

There's nothing I'm afraid of like scared people. —Robert Frost

Because the extraordinary bits fall by the wayside as we pursue the logical, practical, adult.

This book is about reclaiming a creative spirit in your fantastic, unique life. It is about living your whole entire life as art, not just the bits you draw on a canvas or embroider or sing. It is about opening space for random acts of creation. It is about approaching every interaction as a grand blank canvas for art to break out. If you're alive, you're creative. If you're alive, you're an artist.

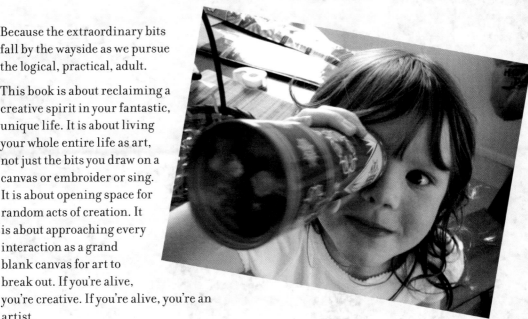

Does the world need another book about creativity? Maybe not. Probably not. No. But I had one I needed to write—one from a different perspective than many "creativity" books. And that's the point. Putting our voice out into the world isn't for others, not really—it is only for ourselves, ultimately. If it touches someone else, if it changes their life or angers or buoys them, that's not yours to own. Yours is to write, to paint, and to keep on doing that, saying what you long to say.

There are three primary audiences for this book

Each of these three groups has an aspiration—a yearning—and is peeking in the covers of this book to see if it might help them:

I don't have a creative bone in my body and I really wish I were more creative.

I'm just a dabbler but I'd love to be a real artist or craftsperson.

I'm an artist and I would love to be known and respected and be able to support myself with my art.

> ART TEACHES NOTHING EXCEPT THE SIGNIFICANCE OF LIFE.
>
> —Henry Miller

Quick question: Which one are you?

Not creative; a dabbler; or an artist? _____

Which do you long to be? _____

What keeps you from being that? _____

The whole of life lies in the verb *seeing*.
—Teilhard de Chardin

Now, let's reframe these statements. What if your art could provide everything you ever needed or wanted in life? How, then, would you finish the following sentences? I've included my own answers to spark your thoughts:

I am creative because _____

I am creative because I am alive and want to fully explore my deeply artistic spirit. I want to leave a portion of myself behind.

I make art because _____

I make art because it gives me fantastic amazing joy and I can't imagine not creating. I want to leave a portion of myself behind.

I must express my unique vision and find ways to share that vision with others because_____

I must express my unique vision because others might need it in their lives. Even if they don't know they need it. I want to leave a portion of myself behind.

TO LIVE A CREATIVE LIFE, WE MUST LOSE OUR FEAR OF BEING WRONG.
—Joseph Chilton Pearce

Today, I am an artist. —Jean Miller

CHAPTER TWO

Get Messy: How to Use This Book

Creativity requires the courage to let go of certainties.
—**Erich Fromm**

There is no right way to read this (or any other) book. I'll make a few suggestions, but offer you this freedom: There are no rules. What few rules appear to be in place are all made up. Make up your own. Then break those, too.

Write in the broad margins with a silver Sharpie. Keep it pristine without making a mark. Fold pages down. Or don't. Invade it with an army of Post-it notes and paper clips. Rip pages out if you feel so inclined. Read the whole thing at once or just read two pages a day. Do the exercises. Don't do them. Rebel against them. Rant about them. Tell me they're stupid, but only after you come up with an exercise that makes more sense for you.

Here's how I read: I thrash through books, pen in hand, talking back to the pages. I make tiny drawings in the margins, I connect the dots, I make it mine in a way that suits me. That's your charge, too: Read this book and use it in a way that fits your life.

Use words and images to capture your journey to fuller awareness. Break the rules. What rules? Create a safe playpen. Limitations allow creativity to flourish. Creativity isn't a technique—it's a mind-set.

YOU WERE BORN AN ORIGINAL.
DON'T DIE A COPY.

—John Mason

What you'll need

The only equipment you need to work through this book in the way I've envisioned it is two black pens (my choices are the happy Pilot Fineliner and the even happier black Sharpie so you have two different line widths, but maybe

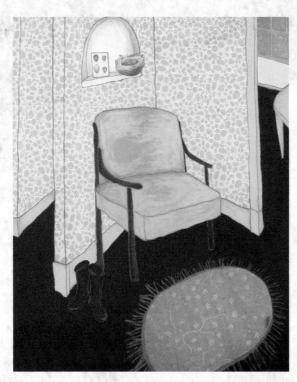

that's just my long-standing pen line fetish coming out), a rather large wad of unlined 3x5-inch index cards (I use white, but, hey, go wild!), a pair of scissors, a glue stick, a timer, some magazines you can cut up, and a rubber band to hold your index cards together. At about the halfway point, you might want to branch out and add a pen in a different color. Or maybe a shoe box to hold all those index cards. Oh, and a crayon or two. No more than an eight-pack. Think you're too sophisticated for crayons? Think again. You will learn to love them. They are some kind of magic.

That's it. Think that's too simple? Too elementary? That's the point. We think creativity needs freedom and lots and lots of crayon colors and the perfect, pristine Moleskine notebook. It doesn't. **Restriction is our friend.** Restrict yourself to just those supplies to work through this whole book and see what emerges. I have a feeling you will surprise yourself. As G. K. Chesterton wrote, "Art is limitation. The essence of every picture is the frame." Your frame is the index card. Enjoy the limitation and see how it frees you.

Magic can happen with just some index cards and a black pen and a crayon. We lose sight of that, I think, in our mania for supplies. Artfulness emerges from simplicity, not from a fully stocked studio. Creativity is internal, not public. At least not at first.

[**I play better tennis because the court is there.**
—Robert Frost]

What this book isn't

This isn't a book about writing the great American novel.

It isn't a book about painting the next *Mona Lisa*.

It's not a book about tools or supplies or the Ten Top Tips for Greater Creativity or the latest way to transfer images onto fabric. And it's not a book about ditching your job as an insurance salesman to be a poet. Wallace Stevens never did that and just look at the poetry the man wrote.

> FOR A LONG TIME I LIMITED MYSELF TO ONE COLOR—AS A FORM OF DISCIPLINE.
> —Pablo Picasso

It isn't a book about impressing people with your ability to do a spot-on life-drawing of Johnny Depp,* or about apologizing for your lack of skill.

It isn't a typical book about creativity.

It isn't a book about any technique at all, because creativity isn't a technique.

It's none of those things, because there's an important conversation we need to have with ourselves long before we get to technique or tools or supplies or shows.

It is a book about nurturing your creative spirit, the one that gets bogged down by paying bills and folding laundry and working for a living. Go too fast into technique and you miss that important uncovering, diving into.

It is a book about turning every day into a joy and color and sound expedition. It is a book about being fully creative simply by being more deeply human and more fully present. Go too fast into technique and you start fixing your vision too soon. Let it expand first. Find rhythms of sound and color everywhere first. Live your fullest, most expansive life first, the one with your eyes (and heart) wide, wide open. Ferociously so.

This is a book about the deeper questions of the ways in which we divide ourselves from our innate creative spirit . . . and how to walk back toward that space in which every instant is a miracle and an inspiration for artfulness, an opportunity for graceful expression of who we are as humans. We long to say something with our lives—what is it? How can we know if we don't open up the window and hear the birds sing?

---

*See? It only took me 13 pages to mention Johnny Depp.

It is a book about seeing the artfulness in everyday life, wherever you find yourself on that continuum between "I don't have a creative bone" and "I'm an artist." It's about seeing life itself as a dramatically, exuberantly creative act.

That's harder than it sounds. And it's easier than we make it.

This is a book about waking up to the beauty around you—the beauty of seeing more and living more deeply. What emerges from that equation is art. Not Art with a capital *A*. That kind of Art scares me because it takes us out of the doing (writing to write, painting to paint) and right into performance, comparison, sales. I'm talking about art with no capital. The art that is your life. Artfulness that only you can create, that is uniquely, incredibly yours.

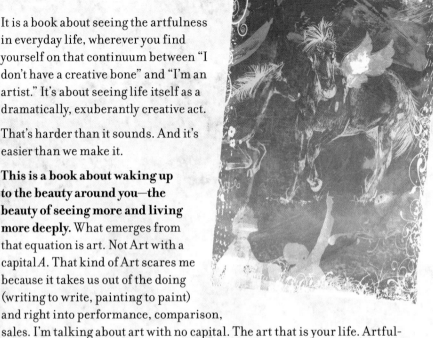

ART IS NOT THINKING SOMETHING UP;
IT IS THE OPPOSITE—
GETTING SOMETHING DOWN.

—Julia Cameron

You'll note brief "Twitter-friendly" summaries of key points on index cards at the start of each chapter. For those who don't "tweet," to use the verb associated with it, Twitter is a popular social media site that limits messages to 140 characters or less—providing the exchange of information in micro-bursts like those you'll find at the start of each chapter. These key points might mirror your learning, and they may not. Cross them out and add your own if need be.

At the end of reading this book, you might have 20 or 37 or 500 index cards on which you've written, scribbled, drawn. Or you might have none. And either way is perfectly fine. Do you get what I'm saying here? THERE IS NO RIGHT ANSWER, no perfect way to work through this book—or through life.

Every single moment of your life is an opportunity for creativity. Even the darkest moments. Perhaps especially them.

Orville Wright did not have a pilot's license. —Gordon MacKenzie

CHAPTER THREE

Embrace the Six Creativity Killers

I plan to write more books whenever I can find the appropriate writing attire and color-coordinated pen. —**Miss Piggy**

My husband, John, sent me this e-mail:

> *Some of America's most iconic writers have produced their greatest works in a short period of time. Herman Melville wrote all of his fiction between 1846 and 1856—eleven books in all, including the magnificent* Moby-Dick, *a book that would take others of us a whole life-time (and more). [My note: Makes me dizzy even to think of it.] In just eight years Faulkner publishes the following six books:* Pylon *(1935),* Absalom, Absalom! *(1936),* The Unvanquished *(1938),* The Wild Palms *(1939),* The Hamlet *(1940), and* Go Down Moses *(1942). [My note: Well, you almost have to hate him for that.]*

> *In just ten years Hemingway published* In Our Time *(1924),* The Torrents of Spring *and* The Sun Also Rises *(1926),* Men Without Women *(1927),* A Farewell to Arms *(1929),* Death in the Afternoon *(1932),* Winner Take Nothing *(1933), and* Green Hills of Africa *(1935). In the thirteen years leading to 1608, Shakespeare wrote twenty-two of his major plays.*

> *Einstein had far-and-away his most outstanding and productive period*

Stop making excuses and start flinging words on a page or paint on a canvas. Don't separate "real" life from "creative" life. Pay attention to your excuses. You are always in choice.

from 1905 to 1915, all sandwiched by the special and general relativity theories. Darwin published five books from 1859 to 1868, including The Origin of Species. *Mozart produced almost half of all of his music in the last ten years of his life (Köchel numbers 315–598), 283 compositions in 3,650 days.*

John was intrigued, he said, by the compactness of their creativity, those short, significant bursts of powerful writing and thinking, those consecutive years of a bright burning spark flaming up, then sometimes out, but we won't focus on that part of the story. The examples abound: J. M. W. Turner, Willa Cather, Hermann von Helmholtz (John's all-time greatest hero), Duke Ellington, Charlie Parker, Carl Friedrich Gauss, Charles Dickens— all of them not just prolific but importantly so. Their work and sounds shaped and changed the world.

Call me crazy, but I'm thinking that all this significant output wasn't because they had finally gotten the 2.4GHz Intel Core 2 Duo MacBook Pro they'd been waiting for and had at last created an office that looked like a Pottery Barn ad. They hadn't put it off until things were more convenient or they finally were able to purchase that Aeron chair they had always dreamed of or invest in that Bedford Smart Technology furniture collection that would "allow me to enhance my home with the modern ease of technology without sacrificing the tradition of comfort and style."

No, their work was driven from some less convenient place inside them, not necessarily by external comfort, acceptance, number of blog readers, awards, or sales, but something else.

Have I come into my profoundly productive period yet? Have you? Will we know when we're in it, or will others look back and see it only in retrospect, as we have with Faulkner and Einstein? Or will it not happen at all because we are waiting until we get that new laptop, until we get our filing system

A hunch is creativity telling you something. —Frank Capra

set up, until we get the kids all grown up, until we get everything else on our to-do list done, or until we acknowledge what makes us burn from the inside out?

These writers and artists and scientists felt a compelling drive from deep inside to say something. What is it that you and I need to say? And in what form? I wonder, if we started today, what might we be able to write or create or make or achieve in the next . . . oh, I don't know . . . the next 37 days? How about the next ten years?

We block ourselves from our creative selves in many ways—by comparing ourselves with others, by setting the bar way too high for ourselves, by investing in a "story" like "all artists are poor," "I can't draw a straight line," or "I can't find my voice."

Six creativity killers

Here are six of the most common reasons people give me that they can't be creative, write a book, paint, or make art. Do you recognize yourself in any of these? Which ones? And which ones would you add?

I can't be creative because . . .

I work full-time.

> My job sucks the life out of me. I'm tired when I come home, so I can't be creative then. I have kids. My partner expects me to spend my free time with him/her, not painting or weaving baskets. I can either make a living or be creative, not both. I need more hours in the day. Sure, she's successful because she

doesn't have kids and doesn't spend her time trying to sew those little badges on a Daisy Scout uniform or attending Little League soccer games. I could make art, too, if I was retired, single, shorter, richer, quieter. I need a trust fund or a nice patron named Medici. I need someone to recognize my brilliance and walk right up to my door with a few million dollars so I can be freed from my cubicle. Nothing short of that will do. I can either have that or just sit here and eat chocolate lava cake. I'll have to wait until that happens. *Then* I can be creative.

I don't have a good space in which to work.

I have no studio—or my studio is too cramped—or my studio is too messy. The light's all wrong. If only I had a writing shed to call my own, I could write that novel. One day I'll have the right space. I need perfect working conditions. I need a tiny island far from everyone who needs me for something. I'll wait until the kids leave for college (let's say they're two years old now) and *then* I'll have the space to work.

I don't have the right materials.

If only I had the right equipment. I don't have the right color paint and the notebook I have is ruled, but I need a blank one. I need a different pen. If I had a different pen, I could write the Great American Novel. One of those nice ones the astronauts use so I can write upside down. If I had that Space Pen, and if it was engraved with an inspirational saying by a famous poet, then I could get published.

YOU CAN'T USE UP CREATIVITY. THE MORE YOU USE, THE MORE YOU HAVE.
—Maya Angelou

I have no ideas.

I can't think of a thing to create. How does she come up with those ideas? I'm an idiot, a dullard, boring. My work, family, PMS, astrological chart, sunburn, all drain the ideas out of my head. I used to be creative, but no more. I don't have an original thought. I've got nothin'. I majored in accounting or psychology, not art. How can I be expected to compete with people who have an MFA?

I don't have any skill.

I need to take more classes. I don't know the right techniques. I'm not trained. I need a degree. I need a BA, MFA, PhD, before I can tackle making something worthwhile. I need someone to tell me what to do. I need a teacher, a mentor, a coach, a guru. I need another book or class before I start. I need to find an answer outside myself.

They won't like it.

People will laugh. They will tell me their children could do better. They won't buy it. They will tell me I'm foolish for even try-

[
The legs are the
wheels of creativity.
—Albert Einstein
]

ing. I am not really doing this for myself, but for others who will judge it. It would be stupid to think I could sell any of these. No one would want to read these stories/look at these pictures. Why create them if nobody's going to buy them? I'll never get a review in the *New York Times* and if I do, it'll rip me to shreds.

Each of these is a story we are busy telling ourselves about ourselves. They are all stories of comparison, perfectionism, or lack. Not good enough, must make better, don't have what I need (time, money, space, materials, ideas).

Which ones are your story?

Do you want that vast, fabulous canvas called your life to be a story of comparison, perfectionism, or lack? You could, but that would keep you out of happy, fulfilled, creative fun. Instead, do you want your life to be a rambunctious story of uniqueness, imperfect beauty, and abundance?

Underneath all these deflections is a belief that our lives are divided into two parts:

The Real Part, and

The Creative Part

Maybe those shouldn't be separated in the way we've been taught.

Maybe the Real Part is the Creative Part. And maybe, just maybe, the Creative Part is the Real Part.

Maybe there's no real separation between them.

Maybe we shouldn't have to lumber through algebra to get to art class. Maybe algebra class should be more artful.

Imagine that.

I recently got a message on Facebook from someone who summed up some of this disconnect between "real life" and "creative" or "intentional" life: "If I had only 37 days," she wrote, "I wouldn't be doing my taxes, I wouldn't be going to work, I wouldn't be worried about all the bills, I wouldn't worry about not having time to go and take pictures or write. But I likely *do* have 37 days. So I must do my taxes. I must go to work. I must worry about the bills. All those things must happen, therefore I don't have time to write or take pictures. And all this is besides my relationship with my husband and two-year-old. I love your philosophy but I just cannot reconcile it with where I am at right now. I've read and quite enjoyed Eckhart Tolle and I know that there is no past, no future, only BE HERE NOW. Fine. That doesn't mean that practical life gets to be ignored so I can paint a masterpiece. Being present is fine, but tomorrow needs to be anticipated and prepared for. Otherwise when it becomes the present it will be a righteous mess!"

CREATIVITY IS A TYPE OF LEARNING PROCESS WHERE THE TEACHER AND PUPIL ARE LOCATED IN THE SAME INDIVIDUAL.

—Arthur Koestler

"What if you make your practical life the masterpiece?" I wrote in response.

What if what keeps us out of that deep, rich, redolent source of longing for creative spirit is our either/or way of seeing the world?

I can either be a mother or a writer.

I can either do the dishes or paint a masterpiece.

I can either be an executive or a sculptor.

I can either be fully bursting with the joy of life or be practical.

I can either be an insurance salesman or be a poet.

I can either teach yoga or be wealthy.

What if life is both/and, instead?

I can be a creative mother who creates each school lunch like it was
a wee masterpiece, a Cézanne in a
hemp Fair Trade lunch bag, simply
because it makes me over-the-moon
happy to do so.

> I ALWAYS WAIT FOR INSPIRATION TO WRITE.
> IT ARRIVES EVERY MORNING AT 9 A.M.
>
> —Peter DeVries

I can sculpt my leadership style, imbuing my management meetings with
a quote about creativity at the top of each agenda, including a section in my
board book that provides staff and board members with food for thought
from Melville or Charlotte Perkins Gilman or poet-activist Andrea Gibson.

I can imbue my practical life with bursts of joy, walking out my front door
every Monday in search of the color red, documenting with a digital camera
or a hash mark on the back of my hand when I see it.

I can write poetry on the backs of insurance claims, on Post-it notes at my
desk in my cubicle. I can post a new quote on my computer screen every morning to buoy me. "Write it. Write. In ordinary ink on ordinary paper," begins a
haunting poem, "Hunger Camp at Jaslo" by Wislawa Szymborska. What if we
just write in ordinary ink on ordinary paper on each ordinary day?

**What's the alternative, really, if you don't want to die with your song
inside you?**

As I worked recently with a group of educators in Hastings, Nebraska, one
said in frustration, "Well, we can only do so much. Some children come from
circumstances that we'll never change—they come from lives outside school
that are so desperate and in which the bullying behaviors we're trying to
change are exactly the ones being taught to them by their parents and relatives. We can't change that."

"What's the alternative, really?" I asked. "Do you just throw up your hands
and say, 'I can't do anything about it'? Or do you influence what you can, help

how you can, build relationships as you can?"

We can either own our circumstances (some children live in unhealthy, bullying situations outside school; our time is limited because we have to work or we have children ourselves; we don't have money to take fancy writing retreats) and be creative in them (do what we can to be supportive while they are in school; reserve just ten minutes a day for writing or painting—just ten; go to the library and get *Bird by Bird* or *Writing Down the Bones* and let it be your retreat), or we can throw up our hands and say *I cannot be held accountable because the conditions are not ideal.*

Honey, sugar pie, the conditions will never be ideal. Those are the conditions. Make peace with the conditions: Time feels limited (it isn't, really—we have all the time we need every day right up until the day we die); people are pulling at our apron strings (we train people every day how to treat us—and we can retrain them); we don't have the right materials (do you know how to speak and write a language? You're all set to be creative). You get the idea.

We are always in choice. We may not choose the circumstances, but we can choose how we are in them. Always. We can *always* choose both/and.

Imagine a world in which our practical life *is* the artful life, a world in which the way we place food on our plates is artful (if we all lived in Japan, we would understand that innately). Imagine a world in which each piece of correspondence holds the promise of loveliness; in which business meetings are not divorced from artfulness but imbued with it. It's so easy to rush through dinner, correspond only through e-mail or Twitter, and scoff at the idea that art has anything to do with business. If we finish our work or get the kitchen cleaned to within an inch of its life, we believe, then we might give ourselves to making art. That day might never come. Correction: That day will never come.

This book is an exploration of our stories of lack *(I need),* **our stories of comparison** *(they won't),* **and our stories of self** *(I don't* and *I can't).*

I'm not an expert in creativity. In fact, I know nothing about it. You won't find tips and techniques and how-tos here, though the exercises at the close of each essay might spark new questions and new thinking in you. The only thing I know is how I see the world; in these pages, you'll find that. Along with some questions that I hope will open space for your own discoveries of how you see the world. That's all. And that's everything.

give yourself 10

At the end of each story in this book, you'll find a "Give Yourself 10 [minutes]" challenge. If you're inclined to do the suggested exercises to embed the story's meaning into your own creative life, spend just ten minutes after reading each story either doing what's suggested or creating your own ten-minute exercise—or spend the ten minutes reflecting on what you've read and how it might apply to your amazing life.

You'll use your index cards for these "Give Yourself 10" exercises. One side of the card will be some kind of writing prompt (**Word**) and the other side will be a visual prompt (**Image**). Don't freak out on me here and tell me you're not (1) a writer; or (2) an artist. You are. You have the tools—language and images, whether they spring directly from your forehead onto the index card or you search through all those *O* magazines you've been stock-piling in color-coordinated glory for years now and cut out pictures to glue-stick onto your index card.

An artist cannot fail; it is a success to be one. —**Charles Horton Cooley**

What bar are you setting for yourself? This fantastic amazing brain and soul of yours? *IT HAS THINGS TO SAY AND DRAW.* I feel certain you can find a way to express them. Yes, you surely can.

give yourself 37

You'll also find "Give Yourself 37 [days]" exercises after each story. These are longer-term commitments over 37 days. You'll also use your index cards for these exercises over a longer period of time, to fully explore what the lessons of the story might mean for your own artful life.

Why 37 days? The event that sparked my writing my blog, 37days, and my book, *Life Is a Verb,* was an event just 37 days long. In October 2003, my step-father was diagnosed with lung cancer, and he died just 37 days later. It was shocking, that time frame, and it prompted me to ask every morning, "What would I be doing today if I only had 37 days to live?" What I learned is that every day is day one. And that we almost never know when day 37 will come, but that a life can be changed in that short time frame.

Practice over time is how things change in our lives. Sure, once in a while there is a revolution, a sudden change, a snap in the fabric of the universe, altering life as we know it, irrevocably. But mostly we wake up every morning in the same room looking at the same crooked picture on the wall and life moves on quite incrementally, one leg at a time, one waffle a day, one school lunch after another. That's the magic!

If you do anything—anything—for 37 days straight, your life will change. It will. Life is incremental that way. But in this fast-paced "SIX-PACK ABS IN 3 MINUTES!" culture, it's hard to

The best way to have a good idea is to have lots of ideas. —Linus Pauling

dedicate 37 days to anything. We want those six-pack abs *now.* I get that. And yet . . . I know in my heart of hearts it doesn't work like that. Change is sometimes very small, and hardly noticable, and even discouraging.

Change is that terrible, scary, and fantastic place between insight and action. Sometimes it's hard. Often. It's swimming upstream. It's giving up the excuses we've used thus far to keep ourselves from changing (and that's hard because we've finely honed those excuses over many years, usually, and we're used to them, thank you very much).

LIFE IS AN EMPTY SQUARE UNLESS ONE FILLS IT UP WITH MATTER.

—Robin Antar

Note on these index cards what keeps you out of intention as much as you note your successes. Those patterns are important. So I want to get fit, but if I can't achieve my ridiculously over-reaching fitness goals for today, then I might as well eat chocolate lava cake.

I want to write for three hours a day, but today I only have ten minutes to myself, so I give up being a writer altogether. I fling my hands in the air and perform the "woe is me, I have a job, children, partner, sinus problems, hangnails" poem that I've practiced for years. Those are patterns of investing in the story of the obstacle instead of investing in the story of the yearning. What are your patterns? You'll explore them through these pages.

For those who appreciate what happens when you create in community, you can find information at www.pattidigh.com on how to post images of your index cards in our ongoing shared journey as a VerbTribe.

[Most of us go to our grave with our music still inside us.]
—Oliver Wendell Holmes

PART TWO
The Six Creative Commitments

Fear is the reason for making art.

It is a means to freedom.

—*Ilya Kabakov*

irreverent baking

I should be upstairs with the others, drumming up ways
to heal the world, save the animals, pray for water
in a far-off continent, devote the remainder of my days
to a catalog of restorations. But this morning, it was the matter
of scones that drew my gaze, and my feet remained
planted in the kitchen. One must never ignore the instinct
to create, is what I told myself, and soon the counter was stained
with flour, my hands sticky with dough, the house inked
with the smell of blueberry possibility, and I knew I was not wrong.
This was my prayer, my act of healing, my offering, my song.

—*Maya Stein*

What can we do to reclaim our creative spark, to see the world through a child's eyes again, to see art in the smell of blueberry possibility?

We are telling ourselves stories every moment, storying ourselves in order to make meaning of what is happening around us. Since **we are always in choice** (we might not choose the circumstance, but we choose how we are in it), why not create a story of abundance rather than lack, one of generosity rather than scarcity, of embrace rather than fear, of collaboration rather than comparison, of both/and instead of either/or, of resources rather than commodities, and of community rather than the individual alone?

Why not? We have to unlearn in order to do that. It flies in the face of a culture hell-bent on best-seller lists and page rankings and shiny gold Oscars and "buy by midnight tonight to get a bamboo steamer" sales and marketing techniques.

Stop all that. Those are the very things that block us from our own creative well.

Step away.

Quiet your mind.

[We can't be creative if we refuse to be confused. —**Margaret Wheatley**]

Focus on the direction of your intention—is it generative, positive, sharing . . . or is it reductive, negative, and grasping?

We have to unlearn those reductive, negative, grasping behaviors, ones ultimately born out of a story of lack. As Gloria Steinem has said, "The first problem for all of us, men and women, is not to learn but to unlearn."

What, then, are the practices and behaviors that honor and enhance our creative spirit rather than further reduce it? There are six, each outlined and illustrated in the chapters to come, each so simple—and yet so difficult.

Here's the Twitter summary of each of the six creative commitments:

Be ordinary: Put down your clever. Get lost more often. Be confused.

See more: Turn around and look. Slow down long enough to really see. Pay attention.

Get present: Show up like magic. Be fully here now. Follow the thread.

Catch fire: Please lick the art. Live like your hair's on fire. Leap!

Clear ground: Stop trying so hard. Simplify. Just do to do.

Let go: Ignore all the critics. Stop all the measurement. Detach from outcome.

CHAPTER FOUR

Be Ordinary: Put Down Your Clever

What we play is life. —**Louis Armstrong**

I was hired recently to give a keynote speech to a nonprofit association that was meeting in Austin, Texas. A few days before I left for Austin, I looked up their conference program online to get a sense of the rest of the meeting, and how my speech on *Life Is a Verb* might fit in.

"Oh, no!" I yelled from the dining room to John, who was in the family room. He came running, thinking I had hurt myself somehow. "LOOK AT THIS," I said rather loudly. "THE KEYNOTE SPEAKER THE DAY BEFORE—LOOK AT WHO IT IS!"

He looked. "So?" he said. The speaker was the first American and the first woman to row solo across the Atlantic Ocean.

She rowed across the ocean.

"SO?" I said. "What on earth could I possibly say that would be as exciting as rowing across AN ENTIRE OCEAN? My stories are little—SHE ROWED ACROSS AN OCEAN. I bet she has videos and lived through storms. She's going to tell this incredible adventure story and then I'm going to get up the next day and talk about Tess walking around with a tiny grape in her hand."

Everyday, mundane life is the work.
Be easy in your own skin.
Stop being so smart.
Make daily commitments
to showing up as you are.
Don't stand in your own shadow.

A poem only lives when it has a soul to reside in. —**Julius Lester**

I was distraught by the comparison.

John looked at me and then said, quietly, "I didn't realize this was a competition."

I flew to Austin thinking about the ways in which we discount our ordinary and the ways in which we compare ourselves with others. I realized up there in the wild blue sky at 37,000 feet above where we should be that raising two children was at least as hard as—if not much harder than—rowing solo across the Atlantic.

One of the primary tenets of improv that my business partner, David Robinson, taught me very early in our work together is to "put down your clever, and pick up your ordinary." We keep ourselves out of our creative spirit by trying to be smart, to know, to be clever and "with it" and anticipate the answer that "Teacher" wants—whether that is an actual teacher, or a boss, or a partner. As David says, **we are at our most potent at our most ordinary, but we can't see it.** Because it's our ordinary, we believe it's everyone's ordinary.

It's not.

My "ordinary" is unique to me. But because it is just how I see the world, I discount it, minimize it, believing there must be another, faster, better, more clever, quick, and funny way to see the world. We compare ourselves with others and in that single action, we are lost to our own creative spark, the one that exists outside the world of measurements against others.

ARGUE FOR YOUR LIMITATIONS AND, SURE ENOUGH, THEY'RE YOURS.

—Richard Bach

As John said of my keynote speech, this isn't a competition. How can we put down our clever and pick up our ordinary?

Come as you are

I dip my pen in the blackest ink, because I am not afraid of falling into my inkpot.

—Ralph Waldo Emerson

Miami

Just after *Life Is a Verb* came out, I was asked to give a keynote speech about it to an industry organization I had belonged to for many years. I flew to Miami to give the speech after many "I've got nothin'" conversations with David, and met with the audiovisual technicians at the hotel to see how my PowerPoint slides would work the next morning.

"Wow," they both said as we sat in a cold, darkened hotel ballroom looking at the slides, which were nothing but big projections of the beautiful art from *Life Is a Verb.* No language on them, no spinning and flashing bar charts or pie charts or bullet points. Just art. "These are so beautiful," Jose said to me, and to his colleague. "We never see such beautiful slides," his colleague responded. I explained how readers of my blog had created the artwork, thanked them for their help, and went to my room.

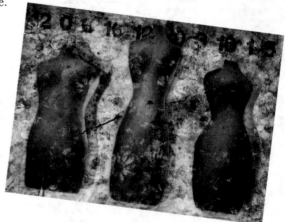

And then it began, that internal chatter in my head: *What was I thinking? This is a professional meeting. I must have words on the slides to reinforce my message, so people will know what to write down, what to remember. I can't just have art—I have to have words. They expect that. Beautiful art is too . . . lightweight or something.* The chatter continued. I called David at his home in Seattle, too many times to admit. And I sat for four hours in that hotel room creating slides to insert into my presentation. Quotes, bullet points, things for the audience to grasp onto, take notes from. Ugly black slides with big white text.

After four hours of working on it, changing it, "professionalizing" it, I looked at the slide show preview. **The beautiful art the AV techs had exclaimed about was completely overshadowed by slides that looked just like fear.** But I was determined to be professional and Twitter-worthy with my quips made concrete in the form of PowerPoint text. Ugly, yes. But safer.

I hit SAVE.

The laptop froze.

Four hours of work were lost.

When I realized it, I had a moment of panic, and then laughed a long, long laugh. *Ah,* I remember thinking. *The universe is saving me from myself.* I closed my laptop and spoke using the art slides the next morning—and at every presentation since.

> HUMAN POTENTIAL IS THE SAME FOR ALL. YOUR FEELING, "I AM OF NO VALUE," IS WRONG. ABSOLUTELY WRONG. YOU ARE DECEIVING YOURSELF.
>
> —Dalai Lama

Sturbridge

Before going to Sturbridge, Massachusetts, I had put a call out on Twitter for help. No local bookstore could be found by my publisher to help with book sales after my speech, so I took to the airwaves to find someone who would help sell books in exchange for a book and dinner. Artist Gwyn Michael responded. She would be visiting family about 40 miles from Sturbridge and would be happy to help. We made arrangements, and I set out on my journey a week later.

Because of my experience in Miami, I opted to just show up, to just come as I was to this group of 300 people. I sat on a stool on the stage and simply talked and read. It was a revelation to me—they responded in magical ways to the truthfulness and simplicity of what I had offered. We sold out of books quickly. It was a big lesson in just showing up.

I took Gwyn to dinner, joined by another Twitter and blog friend I had never met, a man named Steve Sherwood. Steve and I listened as Gwyn told *her* story of that day. Just after she agreed to help me, she said, she panicked. "I'm an artist," she told us, "I didn't have the right clothes. I decided I couldn't come in my blue jeans, which is what I wear every day to make my art, but that I needed to go out and buy a suit or some kind of professional dress to fit in and be appropriate at the conference."

Sound familiar? I smiled to myself at the table, with a sense of knowing.

She went out and bought an outfit to wear. "But when I got it home," she went on, "I hated it. It was itchy. It didn't feel like me. I just agonized about it, and finally realized I needed to take that outfit back and come as I am."

Two identical messages had come to us from different events but at the same time and in the same place. I toasted Gwyn, toasted synchronicity, and told my story.

What might happen if your ordinary is enough? If you don't need to be more professional, cute, appropriate, smart, fill in your own blank? **What if, in fact, you are your most potent when you just come as you are**, without hiding behind spinning PowerPoint slides, without an itchy suit, without fanfare, without the latest journaling or soldering or painting techniques in your arsenal? Just you. On a stool. Telling your story (in words or images). Show up as who you are.

give yourself 10

Word: What do you need to put down in order to be fully present and "ordinary"? Completing this sentence might be a helpful start to this writing: *I need to be more* _____. Maybe that blank is filled with exactly the "clever" you need to put down.

Image: What image can you create (draw, collage) that represents you when you "come as you are"?

give yourself 37

For 37 days make note of the comparisons that come up, both inside your head and out loud. Make note of the times you believe you need to be more _____. Just become acutely aware of the ways in which you believe you must move beyond your simple, beautifully human self to the Queen or King of All He Surveys. It happens more often than you realize, most likely. For each of those moments you've made note of, ask yourself this question: *What else might be true?* For example, if you believe you need to be more creative, it might also be true that you are fully creative and simply need to let go of the measurement you've set for yourself about what "creative" is in order to allow that art spark to flourish. If you say, "I need to be more _____," then say, "I am fully _____, and need to use that power to do _____." Act your way into your ordinary power.

Leave your base camp

Money often costs too much. —**Ralph Waldo Emerson**

Last Tuesday I found myself in the unusual position of being at the very top and very bottom of Maslow's Happy Hierarchy of Needs at exactly the same time.

Typically when I've been making a good living, the money has been accompanied by varying degrees of feeling an imposter and, well, feeling more than slightly miserable or oddly disengaged at the same time—like those descriptions of people having out-of-body experiences while floating above their deathbed. A tad disconcerting given my fear of heights, but mainly just numbing rather than debilitating.

For years I was paid well for work that didn't connect me to my Self in any real way yet was externally validated and accomplished: books published with an odd sense of disconnect from them, speeches given that further commodified a business-speak providing no real value to the world—blah, blah, blah, Fido, blah, blah, blah, Fido—bios that impressed but didn't feel real somehow, newspaper clippings that mothers collect and laminate so they can whip them out at the beauty shop and class reunions to impress their friends. Oh, sure, good work was done in there; but was it really me doing it, or the surface of me, leaving the inside part to just hang out or hang on, waiting to scale the pyramid?

So here I am now, simultaneously at the pinnacle of self-actualization (The Top) and the depths of "financial creativity" (The Bottom). There's a simple explanation for that, of course—it takes a while for new work in the world to take root. But forget the bottom part for the moment, I've just never reached that top before now—I've been stuck somewhere in the middle for the past twenty years. Lots of good stuff in that middle, for sure, but hey, it's a whole new Mount Everest that I've climbed lately. It was time to climb farther after twenty years of base camping.

The view from up here, well, it's spectacular! No wonder those frostbitten climbers make their way to Mount Everest or Machu Picchu and peaks beyond—it's just bloody amazing up here! **I never knew I wasn't here until I finally got here**, like people tell you you'll just know when you go into labor and you can't know what they mean until you actually do know, an infinite regress of knowing only when knowing, being only when being, recognizing the peak only when peaking.

I've never thought so clearly—the air is so clean and true and easy to move through, like the weightlessness of the moon, Neil Armstrong and me just prancing along, bouncing on the surface, hardly weighted down, knocking back some Tang. What's more, my arias sound amazing up here, like I've found my one true voice, ringing out over the moon rocks. Wow. If I close my eyes and sing, I sound like Denyce Graves or Barbra Streisand on a good day when you can see forever—strong and sure and clear. It's exhilarating and liberating and redeeming, this stronghold I have at the top of the world. And yet, hello, hello, hello, here I am, near the bottom, too, my voice echoing in the depths, like a spelunker in a dark, wet cave. (Let me go on record as saying that I don't do bats, not since one stalked me in my apartment in Charlottesville for three nights, me fending it off from underneath an ironing board.)

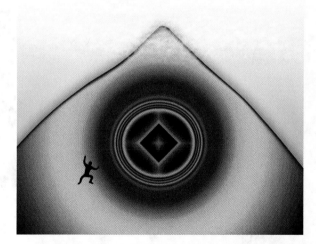

Starting a fantastic new business venture, writing in my real voice for once, hoping to find a way to hold open the space to do the best work of my life—which I know it is—and keep afloat while doing it, until people find it and want it. Work that isn't for everyone, but for some it will make the difference, both personally and organizationally. Work that I'll no longer apologize for. Work that feels so good, and offers such very good hiking buddies as I make my way up the pyramid face.

I'm not at the very bottom, not compared with many in this world, no. But the view from where I am down here is a different one from the middle or the top, a place for questioning whether it's true—like they say—that if you do what you love, the money will follow.

(Look, I don't mean to be picky or move too quickly through the doing and loving to the money, but I do have a few questions about that Happy Hypothesis: About how soon does that money follow? And is it following in a straight line? Should I do a Mapquest to help it find its way? Is it stuck at the border somewhere, a victim of the Homeland Security Act? Has it been held up for questioning?)

Perhaps the gap wouldn't seem so big if the work weren't so right, so worth the stretch across that abyss, the mile-high bridge. I just know that I can't go back down; rappelling is out of the question. And maybe most entrepreneurs feel this awkward juxtaposition of top and bottom simultaneously when they are following their dream.

I know from Maslow that when needs are unmet, our physiological needs take the highest priority. So my fear is that my needs at the bottom will keep me from staying and playing at the top, that I will deflect that work and go for safety, that I will not be able to hold open that space to be creative, that I will fall prey to the American adoration of the short term, that I will dive from this peak.

I REALIZE THAT IF I WAIT UNTIL I AM NO LONGER AFRAID TO ACT, WRITE, SPEAK, BE, I'LL BE SENDING MESSAGES ON A OUIJA BOARD, CRYPTIC COMPLAINTS FROM THE OTHER SIDE.

—Audre Lorde

Maslow's pyramid has five steps, starting at the bottom:

1. Physiological—**I'm comfortable.**

2. Safety—**I'm safe.**

3. Love—**I belong.**

4. Esteem—**I'm respected.**

5. Self-Actualization—**I'm me.**

Those are his steps—and yours and mine. But it's far too easy to stay on Step 4, isn't it? To stay there and think we've reached "I'm me" when we've only reached "I'm respected," achieving the respect of others, not our own. And (sorry, Mr. Maslow) Step 4—esteem—really comes in two versions: the need for the respect of and recognition by others, and the need for self-respect. They aren't at all the same—and isn't it the confusion of the two that leads us to have those out-of-body experiences in the first place, always aiming to please others, not ourselves?

> THE MORE FRIGHTENING THE WORLD BECOMES . . . THE MORE ART BECOMES ABSTRACT.
>
> —**Wassily Kandinsky**

There, at the apex of his pyramid in that misty clouded peak, is self-actualization, the instinctual need of humans to make the most of their unique abilities. As Maslow described it, "A musician must make music, the artist must paint, a poet must write, if he is to be ultimately at peace with himself. What a man can be, he must be. This need we may call self-actualization."

What must I be? What must you? And if we aren't those things, how do we feel? How do we even know it, just as knowing about labor pains really requires being in the throes of them?

Evidently, Maslow tells us, these needs make themselves felt in signs of restlessness. We feel on edge, tense, lacking something, in short, restless. "If a person is hungry, unsafe, not loved or accepted, or lacking self-esteem, it's easy to know what the person is restless about. **It's not always clear what a person wants when there's a need for self-actualization.**"

Ain't that the truth.

Pay attention to your twitchy, restless legs. They're telling you something important. Climbing will help. Leave your base camp.

give yourself 10

Word: Where are you now on that pyramid? What does it look like there? Where is the peak? What does it look like on the peak?

Image: Create an image that is as detailed as it can be about you at the top of your pyramid, that place where you can say, "I'm me."

give yourself 37

Climbers need spotters, people who will keep them safe, help keep the ropes taut and in good working order. Imagine yourself a climber over these 37 days and identify the people and things that provide a foothold for you (not people who provide the answers, but those who are belayers along the way of your climb to your own next step on the pyramid).

If you know your limits, and dwell on the fact, the canvas will remain blank. —Philip Kennicott

Monogram your morning pancakes

You can't make pancakes without breaking eggs. —**Spanish proverb**

My father's birthday is Christmas Day. He has been dead since 1980, dead at fifty-three. Cheated, him and me and my children, and theirs.

And cheated, too, because he was born on Christmas Day. Imagine the cheaty cheat you'd feel if your birthday fell on Christmas, especially as a kid—whatever happened to that other day, the one midyear, where everyone gets together to sing "Happy Birthday" and play Pin the Tail on the Donkey and eat double chocolate layer cake with small sugar trains on top and shower you with gifts and focus on you alone, celebrating the very fact that you were born into the world?

For him, it was all compressed into one relative-heavy day—nothing to look forward to in March or June or August—no, just this one day, his own birth overshadowed by another and, as time went by, overshadowed even more by a large red-suited man with rosacea.

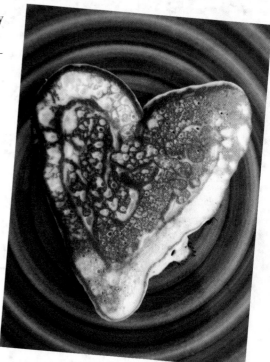

Oh, sure, people would say they had combined your Christmas and birthday present to accommodate both occasions, but I can't imagine that this convenient fabrication made Daddy feel any better, more special, less cheated.

Once he was an adult with a family of his own making, we celebrated Daddy's birthday at Christmas breakfast—specifically focused on his birthday and marred only slightly, I imagine, by the fact that he had to compete for our divided attention—after all, the loot from Santa was achingly just in the next room (my good Lord, man, there's a General Electric Show 'n' Tell Home Entertainment Center Film Strip Viewer and Record Player waiting for me under that tree!)—and perhaps marred also by the fact that he had to cook it himself. Or maybe he wanted to, always having been known as the best breakfast cooker in the house: grits and bacon, sausage and biscuits with sausage gravy, scrambled eggs, pancakes in the shape of animals or letters with Aunt Jemima syrup. (This was before my stubborn descent into vegetarianism as a teenager.)

I loved those pancakes. I adored them. **I loved the attention they represented, the personalized creation of batter and fluff,** perfectly executing a P and a D by his hand and sometimes a flower or a heart or triceratops or the word LOVE.

Grandma would join us, white-gloved to assess the dust; we would put an extra leaf in the table and fold our paper napkins into pointy triangles instead of rectangles, to be fancy. I always thought of it as cozy and realize now that it was actually tight, a table in the small kitchen since we had no dining room, room for only one person to stand and refill juice glasses. Probably my mother dreamed of a house for entertaining the Lottie Moon Women's Bible Study Group; what she got was a house for raising orange-haired children, giving us the biggest room in the house as a playroom complete with a schoolroom-size chalkboard for my work as a pretend teacher and eating, instead, at a table pushed up against the kitchen wall. Never mind that the living room sat unused, ripe for space but untouched by human hands, save when the preacher visited.

So Daddy cooked and we ate, giving him birthday presents at breakfast, wrapped—and this is important—in birthday wrapping paper, not holiday wrap. This couldn't appear a haphazard, forgotten day, lost in the thrill of that Oscar Schmidt Autoharp and new Bobby Sherman album left by Santa, no.

One of those last birthdays (of course, we didn't know how few he had left), I saved all my tips from working at Joe's Dairy Bar and bought my father a Mickey Mouse watch. Mind you, the crowds at Joe's on Sunday nights after church were amazingly large (no lactose intolerance among the Southern Baptist crowd), but cheap, so it took a while to save enough for the special-edition Mickey Mouse watch with the date on the dial! Imagine! I thought it suited his pixie sense of humor, that crooked smile of his, and did he love it!

When he died, I made sure Mr. Sossoman arranged the watch on the wrist on top so all those hundreds of people who came to see him in his satin puffy box would smile and nod knowingly. "Yes," they'd say to themselves, "that Melvin always did have a smile on his face." The funny, bright red "Merry Xmas" western bowtie that he proudly wore with a sly smile to holiday parties is always front and center on my Christmas tree.

That same birthday, I talked Mama into buying Daddy a pair of Lee blue jeans. She balked—"What will people think?"—and I insisted. "He'll love them. Just wait and see."

He wore them every day. He had them on that last harried ride to intensive care on Mother's Day weekend, the unsigned Mother's Day card we found afterward in the trunk of his car a most terrible symbol of his suddenly unfinished life and his thoughtfulness, simultaneously.

Daddy went into the hospital that day and only his clothes came back out. I used to see Mama open that hospital bag of his last clothes, closing its top around the whole bottom half of her face, trying to smell him, desperate for his scent after he went underground. I tried to convince her to also bury him in those loved, worn jeans and his beloved red plaid corduroy shirt, but she drew the line after the Mickey Mouse watch. **A woman knows her limits.** I wear that shirt now and perhaps Mama still has those jeans in that bag, taking them out from time to time for a whiff of him, real or imagined.

Daddy hooked a holiday stocking shortly before he died, having been introduced to the wonders of rug-hooking by a wife who was frantic—desperate even, and with good reason—to provide him with a quiet hobby, one that unlike watching Joe Namath wouldn't involve excitement, anticipation, movement, stress to his heart. If ever there was a hobby like that, I suppose rug-hooking was it, followed only by sleeping.

So when Christmas comes, as it inevitably does, my sadness at his leaving magnifies: when I see that holiday stocking hung from my dining room mantel, I both smile at his leaving it behind and weep for what it represents, a heart patient quietly hooking rugs at the very prime of his life.

Pancakes made into initials—is there any breakfast food more glorious, more personal, more full of sheer, fantastic, lasting love?

Cook monogrammed pancakes for people you love. Wear comfy jeans and a plaid shirt and a goofy watch that makes you (and others) smile. Celebrate your birthday whenever you get a hankering to. Hook a rug to leave behind. **Make art from loss.**

give yourself 10

Word: List the small gifts of the people around you (like monogrammed pancakes) that you overlook because you've called them "little." What creative acts do you see others perform within the context of their "practical" lives?

Image: Make images of those little gifts to remind yourself to use the canvas you're given, whether that is pancakes or a job as an executive.

give yourself 37

What are your "little gifts"? Give away one of them each day as a daily ritual—chances are that they are your "ordinary," so you don't see those gifts as special. They are, to someone else. Make a note of the giving—and give up any attachment to how those "little gifts" are received.

I AM INTERESTED IN MAKING THE SIMPLE PROFOUND, SO MY OWN BACKYARD CAN BE INSPIRATIONAL. I JUST WALK OUT MY DOOR AND IT'S ALL THERE. BY PAINTING SIMPLY, MAGIC HAPPENS.

—Peter Fiore

Learn how to learn

The answer to how is yes. —**Peter Block**

Way back when I was learning my ABCs, names of state capitals, and the preamble to the US Constitution at happy Hillcrest Elementary School way up there on the crest of that hill, We the People of These United States weren't offered the chance to take a foreign language. No, I had to wait until the ninth grade when all those chatty and sparky synapses were concretized, making it almost impossible to create unusual, new sounds and different ways with sentences construct word order to.

Good instructional strategy, that.

In that Dark Insular Age (as opposed to our current Transparent Yet Still Insular Age), the only language offered was French. Mais oui! Given the Massive and Unrelenting immigration of wine-swilling Frenchies to the hills of North Carolina, that mono-lithic linguistic choice made perfect sense, didn't it? Mais non!

I was suspicious that my ninth-grade French teacher might have taken only one French class, sometime in her life. Or not. It became abundantly clear that we wouldn't be confused with native speakers after a year of listening and responding aloud in our sweet southern drawls to her precious, scratchy 33⅓ record of odd French phrases ("A what?" my daughter just asked. "A record?"). Indeed, come to think of it, I've never been asked to join the French Foreign Legion and I suspect that Mme. Brown is to blame.

The first time I crossed the big pond and went to Paris, I was proud to amaze and, I feel it's quite fair to say, delight the good people of the City of Lights with my command of their language. "Il est au zoo!" I exclaimed with merry abandon. "Il est au zoo!" "What do you think of our museums?" my host asked over wine. "Il est au zoo!" "What are the most pressing problems in American corporations today?" one of the delegates at our meeting asked. "Il est au zoo!" I exclaimed loudly! "Is your CEO join-ing us this evening for dinner?" someone asked. "Il est au zoo!" I replied enthusiastically.

"He's at the zoo." That's the single phrase I remember from Mme. Brown's "French" class. And trust me, this is not a phrase that comes up often in conversation. No, I had to work really hard to find opportunities to use it, even badly. The whole thing made me feel a bit like William Burroughs in his happy drug days chopping up pages of text on a tiny guillotine and throwing them into a circulating fan to see what fell where. I pretended I was an Avant Garde poet or Peter Sellers in *Being There,* my idiot savant messages too poignant, too powerful, too precious for comment or explanation.

Following in the Grand Tradition of Useless, Inexplicable, and Inapplicable Knowledge, I learned how to say "There's a small brown dog" in Russian from the disembodied voice of a woman I could only imagine was knocking back frozen pepper vodka and caviar between breathless renditions of this remarkable phrase. Need I tell you that it's tough to find a way to use that phrase while in Moscow on business?

My Russian hosts worked hard to find a small brown dog so I could show off my considerable linguistic prowess. Finally on my last afternoon there, we settled on a big brown slightly militaristic dog in Red Square. It would have to do; evidently the small brown ones were in hiding for the winter. "Будет малая коричневая собака!" I yelled, "Будет малая коричневая собака!" One tiny boy ran screaming toward his mother; others just stared, mouths agape, and the soldiers suddenly stood up straight, cocking their Russian Tokarev M1940 semiautomatic rifles in anticipation.

I realized from those two linguistic fiascos that information isn't terribly useful unless you have a larger framework and context in which to put it,

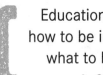

Education ought to teach how to be in love always and what to be in love with.
—A. Clutton Brock

In places like universities, where everyone talks too rationally, it is necessary for a kind of enchanter to appear. —**Joseph Beuys**

use it, apply it, alter it, frame it, change it. **Learning *one thing* is not useful. Learning *how to learn about that one thing* is.** Perhaps that marks the difference between mindlessness and mindfulness, between idiocy and fluency, or between buying tourist souvenirs and being on the short end of a firing squad.

Sometimes when I teach about cultural differences, I fear I'm channeling Mme. Brown and her scratchy recording in that room with no air and small desks. What I want students to learn is not specifics like "zoo" and "dog," but what culture really is, that way of sense-making and meaning-making around common "dilemmas" in the world, and how our answers to those questions vary around the globe. But what they want instead of all that complicated stuff is how to hand their business card to someone in Tokyo, which countries consider it an insult to show the sole of your shoe, and what white flowers symbolize in China or Argentina.

I'm thinking that the need to know deeper isn't true just of cultural or linguistic knowledge, either. Is it useful or dangerous to know a fact if you don't really know why or what that fact illuminates deep down? Is information transferable? Is context important? Is knowing how to think about something as important as thinking about something? Is the concept of culture itself more important than knowing the "10 tips" for business success in Prague? And even before answering any of those questions, must I know my own cultural "answers" before studying those of other people?

Learning things on the surface of life—whether a language or art techniques—doesn't help me with the parts that are deeper down: how people think and think differently, how they make sense of what happens around them, how meaning is made around their dining room table that is different from my dinnertime conversations over mac and cheese (homemade with a garlicky oat topping), how art shows up in their everyday lives. How else does this play out in life? I learn one recipe, but have no idea how to make substitutions; I can play the piano but only with sheet music. *Maybe I can answer the multiple-choice questions of life, but never, ever the essays.*

Learning a formula or phrase or technique limits rather than increases my ability to navigate real life. If that exact situation doesn't arise—if he isn't at the zoo and if there isn't a small brown dog—if I run out of cumin or cinnamon, if someone asks me to play "Frosty the Snowman" instead of the theme song to *Spongebob Squarepants*—then I'm lost, unable to make sense. What if a big white dog shows up or he's at the museum instead of the zoo? I'm illiterate and impotent and ineffective, then. I can't transfer the knowledge to any new situation; I'm stuck.

The students in an undergraduate course I'm teaching this semester are studying about culture and its impact on leadership. After reading Hall's *Beyond Culture* and Nisbett's *The Geography of Thought,* one student said she felt sorry for all those group-oriented people in Asian cultures because they must have no self-esteem and feelings of self-worth. After I nodded that nod that you nod when you're trying to figure out how on earth to answer, I realized that her statement was actually a fantastic representation of how we usually see the world—looking at other people's outsides from our insides.

Well, I explained, they do have self-esteem and self-worth—they just get theirs from being a member of a group while you get yours from being an individual, happily confusing the student's own cultural norm about what self-esteem means and is. How much more important was that thought process than her simply learning that many Asian cultures are group-oriented and being able to answer a multiple-choice question about that?

"Learning to paint" is probably the worst thing that can happen to an artist. —Warren Criswell

The myth that life is simple undermines learning. Embrace the complexity. Don't fall prey to the illusions of right answers, but go beneath the phrases to the meaning below. Don't learn to hand your business card to a Japanese CEO; learn about how people in high-context cultures make meaning instead. Don't memorize one recipe to make when your in-laws come over for dinner; learn how flavors work together. Don't look for a small brown dog; learn how to look for meaning and commonality and community instead. Don't just go to the zoo.

give yourself 10

Word: What "how" questions do you have? How can I learn a foreign language, how can I make the perfect soufflé? How can I be more creative? How can I improve my soldering technique? List them. Now turn each one into a "why" question instead.

Image: Create an image in which for one of these questions the word *how* becomes the word *why*. And in which *why* becomes, simply, *yes*.

give yourself 37

List the things you are seeking answers for outside of yourself—from books, seminars, coaches, et cetera. What are you seeking that you need to identify inside you? What keeps us out of complexity is the belief that we're right. What do you believe you are right about? List those things. And then challenge them by asking *What else might be true?* In this way, try to get confused every day for 37 days, lost in a place of not-knowing.

WHEN ELEMENTARY SCHOOLS INCLUDE ART PROGRAMS IN THE CURRICULUM, CHILDREN DO BETTER WITH MATH.

—Kelly Borsheim

Wear a paper dress

And so our mothers and grandmothers have, more often than not anonymously, handed on the creative spark, the seed of the flower they themselves never hoped to see—or like a sealed letter they could not plainly read. —**Alice Walker**

First, let me just say that I appreciate my mother for so very many things—the whole giving-birth-to-me piece; always telling me that I could be anything I wanted to be; never failing to give me the last mini chocolate éclair, even if she really wanted it; allowing me to plaster my bedroom walls with *Tiger Beat* magazine posters of Bobby Sherman; forgiving me for setting the house on fire (twice, but the second time really wasn't my fault); letting me go by myself to live in Sri Lanka as an exchange student when I was sixteen, even though she was scared to death at

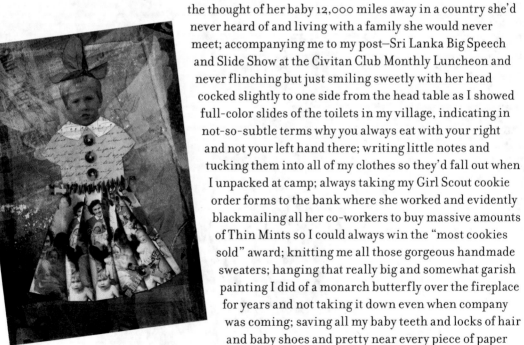

the thought of her baby 12,000 miles away in a country she'd never heard of and living with a family she would never meet; accompanying me to my post–Sri Lanka Big Speech and Slide Show at the Civitan Club Monthly Luncheon and never flinching but just smiling sweetly with her head cocked slightly to one side from the head table as I showed full-color slides of the toilets in my village, indicating in not-so-subtle terms why you always eat with your right and not your left hand there; writing little notes and tucking them into all of my clothes so they'd fall out when I unpacked at camp; always taking my Girl Scout cookie order forms to the bank where she worked and evidently blackmailing all her co-workers to buy massive amounts of Thin Mints so I could always win the "most cookies sold" award; knitting me all those gorgeous handmade sweaters; hanging that really big and somewhat garish painting I did of a monarch butterfly over the fireplace for years and not taking it down even when company was coming; saving all my baby teeth and locks of hair and baby shoes and pretty near every piece of paper I've ever written anything on. And much, much more.

She's always the first person I call when I have good news or bad news, and I imagine that even when I'm eighty years old she'll still remind me to call her when I get home from a trip so she can rest easy and not worry that I had lost control of the car, driven off the highway down a steep incline, and flipped upside down into a vast abyss so overgrown with poison ivy that people won't find me for months unless she knew I was missing. (Shall we just say that she has a vivid imagination for tragedy?)

There's so much to be thankful to Mama for—so please don't get me wrong when I say that I will Never, Ever, Ever, Ever forgive her for letting me go out of the house with one particular choppy pixie-gone-bad hairdo (if you can even call it that) and those eyeglasses, which she picked out for me at an actual Optical Shoppe even though they looked like they were salvaged from the Rotary Club's Eyeglasses Drive for Unfortunate Nearsightedness. What on earth was up with those bangs and ear covers, I ask you?

Enough said, I think.

It really is the small things in life that we remember, isn't it? Either those daily micro-abrasions that scar us (afore-mentioned hairdo) or those clear moments of joy that reso-nate through us like a silver fork on fine crystal, the kind of tone that gets into your bone and thrills you, a lasting one, like that time that Mama, Daddy, my brother, and I went to see a movie together at the Mimosa Theater while it was still daylight out! The year was 1966; I was seven years old. We sat midway down on the left side of the theater, near where I sat years later as a teenager and watched *Tora, Tora, Tora.*

The occasion for this family outing? *The Swiss Family Robinson,* a story of Father and Mother Robinson and their three precious sons—Fritz, Francis, and Ernst—as they fled Napoleon and looked for a place to live in the South Seas. Of course, they are chased by pirates and their ship is pounded mercilessly by the angry ocean. After the ship's crew deserts the sinking vessel, the Robinsons crash on a rocky shore and emerge to find tropical island Eden. Since the ship is filled with food and gear and is only half submerged (how lucky!), they prepare to settle in. The movie was released in 1960; evidently it took six years to make it to my small hometown, or perhaps this was the Swissapalooza Tour, Fritz and the gang serving as backstory to an after-school favorite, *Gilligan's Island.*

To this day, I remember the watering hole that those boys swung over on vines, the ostrich races, and that terrifying moment when little Fritz flailed desperately in the water, fighting the huge man-eating anaconda snake.

More important, I remember (and loved) the fact that Mama came to the movie straight from work, wearing her cat-eye glasses (notice a trend?) and a paper dress decorated all over with bright orange pictures of MasterCharge (now MasterCard) credit cards. Turns out that the bank where she worked had launched MasterCharge that day and all the women had to wear paper dresses—let's hope they were made of Tyvek—to advertise the new service. Hmmm . . . I wonder what the men had to wear?

Paper dresses were quaint inventions of the 1960s and quite fashionable since they were cheap and disposable. Given that I've been known to fix hems with duct tape (and, in a pinch, with a stapler, and—in one memorable

moment—with a paper clip, assuming that even if people noticed, they'd be too polite to say anything), paper dresses were an attractive alternative since you could shorten them with a pair of scissors and mend them with Scotch tape. Even I could do that! And let's be honest, who among us wouldn't want to wear an oversize photo of Pierre Trudeau or the MasterCharge logo to the A&P Food Store? In 1967 *Time* magazine said, "Paper clothing apparently is here to stay." Well, that was evidently before they realized that flammability might be a wee bit of an issue. A small price for beauty, that whole spontaneous-combustion thing.

Because he was such a "catch," Mama has always says she didn't know how she snagged Daddy. Everyone at Calvary Baptist Church was after him, in her version of the story. I can see how that might be true. I think she caught him with her sense of humor, that sly grin and ready laugh that matched his, the way she told stories, that sweet naïveté; I'm sure her flaming red hair and freckles might have had something to do with it, too.

Daddy died when Mama was just forty-seven, a birthday I have passed myself. When I studied in Munich two years after his death, I invited Mama to join me for the final two weeks of the semester. To be honest (but don't tell her), I never thought she would come. After all, she had never even been in an airplane before; there was little chance she'd fly to New York by herself, change not only airplanes but whole airports on her own, fly all night alone, get through customs in Dusseldorf, and land in Munich in a massive snowstorm, was there? I went to the airport to pick her up, half believing she wouldn't be there, but there she was—a testament to the strong part of her that has emerged all through her life and mine when it needed to.

We traveled all over Europe by train in those two weeks, using my room in Munich above the Otto Stuben restaurant at 24 Gabelsburger Strasse as our home base. I took charge, arranging our travel to accomplish her Big Dream: going on the *Sound of Music* tour. The glass gazebo where they sang "I am seventeen, going on eighteen"—or was it sixteen, going on seventeen?—we saw that gazebo. We even stood in it! The cathedral where Maria and What's His Name got married? We were there. While my college friends investigated rumors of hash markets and Red Light Districts in Amsterdam, I escorted Mama around Switzerland, Austria, Germany, and—finally—Amsterdam, proud to show off my cultural negotiation skills.

Mama's friends had told her that she just *had* to try the Swiss fondue, so one icy evening after I had won a side of beef playing bingo in the small inn where we were staying (no, I'm not competitive in the least), we ventured out for fondue. As we ate, I could taste the wine in the cheese; my mother—a Southern Baptist (read: doesn't drink)—widened her significant eyeballs and said, "My, it's getting awfully warm in here!" in her southern drawl as the tiny amount of cooked wine took effect. Afterward, we ventured out in a blizzard, Mama slipping and sliding her way back to bingo, with me holding her up and both of us laughing to the point of tears.

When I was a little orange-haired demon, I don't think Mama had any idea of the creative spark she handed to me, the seed of what flower she had planted in the world, just as I can't quite imagine the flowers my girls will become. Could she see it in my eyes, or was it like a sealed letter she could not plainly read, as she watched me sleep?

For just this one day, I'm going to forgive her for That Hairdo and Those Glasses. Come tomorrow, though, I need some explanations or, at the very least, cash compensation for the trauma I experienced walking in the world looking like that. And while you're at it, you might also try to make up for that Dalmatian dress you made me wear when I was ten.

YOU CAN LEARN AS MUCH—OR MORE— FROM ONE GLANCE AT A PRIVATE SPACE AS YOU CAN FROM HOURS OF EXPOSURE TO A PUBLIC FACE.

—Malcolm Gladwell

Teach me to hear the mermaids singing. —John Donne

The last time he visited, my fabulous friend Tony Frost from South Africa said, "Make a memory today!" to Emma every morning when she left for school. What great advice, how little taken. I think it's hard to predict what those memories will be—which ones will stick and which won't. I think it's just as likely to be a small moment, a paper dress and a midday movie, a bit of fondue and a shared laugh, a Brownstone Front Cake, as it is to be a Great Big Moment where the expectation is too great and the pressure too much and we're trying too hard.

Hand on that creative spark.

give yourself 10

Word: Identify a person who had a great positive impact on you from some time when you were between seven and seventeen years old. Write about that person—what memories does their name evoke, and why? Notice how many of these memories are small gestures, tiny events.

Image: Create an image that represents the spark they provided. What was that spark?

give yourself 37

Each day for 37 days, hand on that spark, however small. Become the person others write about when asked the question above. This happens intentionally, daily, incrementally. Be a memory for someone else.

> YOU ARE TOLD A LOT ABOUT YOUR EDUCATION, BUT SOME BEAUTIFUL, SACRED MEMORY, PRESERVED SINCE CHILDHOOD, IS PERHAPS THE BEST EDUCATION OF ALL.
>
> —Fyodor Dostoevski

Stand on your rock

The map is not the territory. —**Alfred Korzbyski**

A few years ago we took our older daughter to Camp Green Cove, where she spent five and a half weeks rollicking in the woods, riding horses, swimming, hiking and climbing, making friendship bracelets, kayaking, and not writing home.

She'd gone to the same camp the year before, for three weeks that time, and come home changed in some ineffable way—was it the longer hair, the muscles from hiking, the freckles, the new love of salad greens? No, it was something much more than that, the kind of change that makes you cock your head to the side and wonder, but not really know.

Since she hadn't gone to sleep-away camp before, I fretted about her, particularly because she acted so bizarrely when we got there—paralyzed like a doe in headlights, so recognizably freaked out that the counselor asked if we had any medications that we'd like to leave for her at Nurse Nancy's station down by the lake.

"Come on," I said to John after he hauled her heavy trunk to Bunk 8 in Timberline Cabin 2, "we just need to leave and let her get settled," recognizing with a tiny little broken heart that she needed to make this transition on her own and that we were, in fact, the obstacle to her being her own true twelve-year-old self. She felt watched, and perhaps in some way judged, making her even more unsure, an awful tango of anxiety and quiet desperation. More important, **we were a complete embarrassment to her, what with our shirts and pants and shoes and breathing and all**.

"But she can't be embarrassed of us," John cried out in anguish as we made our sad exodus from the camp back into civilization. "I mean, I used to be embarrassed when my parents dropped me off at camp, but those were *my* parents."

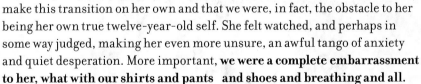

SOMETHING WE WERE WITHHOLDING MADE US WEAK UNTIL WE FOUND IT WAS OURSELVES.

—Robert Frost

Poor, sweet, delusional John.

We are those parents, even if we've read all the Harry Potter books, know who the Teen Titans are, and can sing all the words to Spongebob's theme song *and* "Purple Haze." "Even castles made of sand, fall into the sea, eventually," I reminded him quietly, channeling Jimi Hendrix in my hour of need.

I so feared for shy little Emma. Would she make any friends? Would she come out of her shell? Would she pass her swim test and remember to wear deodorant? Would she flunk cabin inspection? Would she lose her indestructible polycarbonate Nalgene personal hydration water bottle? Would she brush her teeth with any regularity?

[**Strength is a matter of a made up mind.**
—John Beecher]

She seemed so vulnerable, so fragile, so fearful that morning when we left her to join the other girls in microscopic Speedos for their swim test in the frigid lake. We were, for the first time in our lives, totally disconnected from her—no calls, no visits for the first two weeks. I could only rely on her handwritten letters to know she was still alive; every afternoon I felt like a saloon girl in Archer City waiting for the Pony Express to bring news from Little Joe, a highly motivated postal stalker, tracking the mail truck like a scout in the Wild, Wild West reading animal droppings for hire. Thank goodness the camp forced the girls to write a letter home once a week in order to get ice cream on Sunday nights (and by the word *letter*, I mean "sentence") or I would still be tormenting the postal employee who frequents our front porch.

Night after night I fretted, especially during that first week. Knowing that parents across the land were worrying (to be honest, unlike us they were actually probably taking advantage of the solitude by going out for dinner—including appetizers!—like real grown-up people and maybe even seeing movies that weren't rated G or PG—what a concept), the camp set up a section on their Web site where they periodically posted photos of the campers.

I e-mailed the password along to my mother, knowing she would enjoy seeing Emma at camp, too. The site was like crack cocaine, the two of us anxious twins with just the sweetest addiction problem, scouring the Web constantly with a magnifying glass (literally) for even the tiniest of glimpses of Emma, searching for proof that she was, in fact, still alive, having no other evidence of such. We talked ourselves into believing that tiny specks in the distance were Emma hiking, or that the face in shadows at the soulful camp bonfire was hers: "I see her! See Picture B-17, third page, fourth row?

She looks too thin! She's anorexic!" my mother would say. "That's a small tree," I'd reply.

It was the first clear photo of her that we saw on the site that has become an emblem for me of all that is right about finally becoming your own self, of standing tall, of reinventing, of telling your own story about yourself, not the story that has always been told to you or of you. Fearful, shy, quiet Emma had come into her own in just a few days' time. Having signed up for the very first three-day hike that was offered, she conquered, she ruled, she shone from the inside out with a Self Light I'd never seen. In my most honest moments, those moments that both enlighten and appall you, I realized that perhaps she hadn't shone like that perhaps because my own light was too bright and I was casting shadows. And also because I was telling her story as the shy, timid one. And because I was, in subtle and not-so-subtle ways, making her daily decisions for her—a habit, I guess, born of birthing her.

In that first photo, I could see she was Queen of the Rock, Lord of All She Surveys, sure and solid, hands on hips looking squarely into the camera. I half expected to hear Helen Reddy belt out "I am woman, hear me roar" with Aretha Franklin singing backup when I saw this impassioned Declaration of Self R-E-S-P-E-C-T.

She was eager to go back and spend even more time there the next summer, so I spent a week ironing minuscule name tags into her clothing, careful to place them in nonchafing positions because I, like the late Gilda Radner, adhere to the following fashion dictum: Clothing must not itch.

There was mist on the lake the next year when we arrived with our two girls, one too small for camp yet. Emma came armed with a large trunk covered in bumper stickers declaring her love of horses, her fear of clowns, and her vegetarianism, two stuffed manatees, a stuffed bunny, a 6½-inch action figure named Aqualad who bothers me in some indescribable way, a purple sleeping bag, enough shampoo for a preteen platoon, stationery and stamps (hope springs eternal—maybe she can at least sell the stamps for contraband Snickers bars), retro T-shirts with witty sayings on them, and (don't tell her dad) several casually cool outfits for those Saturday nights when the *boys* from the camp across the lake would quietly paddle their manly canoes across its placid surface, that no-man's-land, that symbolic and necessary barrier, to attend the "coeds" (doesn't the beauty of it just make you ache?). In fact, it is the haunting memories of boy–girl sweaty square dance socials (where "square dance" is replaced by "what-I-can't-even-imagine" these days), those beautiful mosquito-riddled frozen instants in hormonal purgatory, that make me so very thankful that I'm in my early fifties sleeping in a real bed with my brilliant and funny and good-smelling husband beside me.

That one photo of Emma on the rock taught me more than I can even say.

Most of the learning is still in the form of questions: What story do we tell ourselves? What stories do we hear others tell about us, over and over and over again—until we start believing them?

What are the stories about ourselves that we don't even tell ourselves, that we never tell others? **What stories about ourselves have we so internalized that we can no longer distinguish the story from the truth?** What stories raise expectations that we spend our lives trying to reach, when—in fact—they aren't really our expectations or our story?

And perhaps most important, what does it mean to be in the shadow of someone else's story—or to put someone else there? How do we do that in subtle ways without realizing it?

Her picture reminded me of how much power there is in being responsible for one's full self, one's own story, stretched tall on that rock.

Emma changed that summer. I hope I did, but I'm not sure. I have to constantly be on guard not to mold her to my story of her, make her what I want her to be or believe her to be, to let her stand on her own damn rock, not mine, play the tuba, not the flute. I have to stop describing her as shy when she isn't, not anymore, no. I have to allow for the growth in her that I want in me. I have to get out of the way and let her get up on that rock.

"What did you eat at camp?" I asked when she begrudgingly returned home, knowing of her pronounced food pickiness and a decided aversion to green vegetables (there was that long-lived and memorable phase of only eating white foods). "Oh, I really *love, love, love* Chef Mike's salad!" she fairly well screamed.

Damn Chef Mike and his homemade buttermilk ranch dressing, I thought to myself, having once fought tooth and nail for Emma to eat a bean (yes, one bean). Or maybe food just tastes better when you're living your life in the sun, hiking and climbing and kayaking all day. Yes, that must be it.

And then, a whole year gone, it was time to get out the magnifying glass again to search for Emma. I'll just look for rocks and I'm sure I'll find her there.

Who is standing behind your rock, in your shadow—is it you? Could you (the "you" of other people's stories) move to the side and **let the real You stand on that rock? Seize your own life narrative! Hop up there!** The view is spectacular.

give yourself 10

Word: What's your rock? Where are you standing in relationship to your "rock"? On it? Behind it?

Image: Draw yourself on that rock. What's your stance?

give yourself 37

Notice every day the stories that you tell about people and about yourself: *My mother is a _____, my boss is a _____, my daughter is a _____, I am a _____.* Catalog as many of these as you can during your 37 days. See which stories you think are accurate. Which do you want to grow past or out of?

Give me a firm place to stand, and I will move the earth. —Archimedes

to see this clearly

I am no magic trick, no doer of miracles, no water walker.
I am no architect of glory, no layer-on of hands, no angel wing.
I am no weaver of gold, no mythmaker, no parachute artist.
I am no halo of stillness in a downpour.
I am no treasure chest, no hero, no thunderbolt wielder.
I am no rabbit foot or lottery number.
I am no combination lock, no mystery ingredient, no optical illusion.
But here is a handful of sunflowers from the florist's sidewalk jungle.
Here is a blanket to spread on the grass for an afternoon.
Here is a song on the radio that calls for dancing.
Here is a chocolate bar I will share with you.
Here is a road sign, a notebook, photographs of those I have loved.
Here is a slice of bright blue sky, a hummingbird
thrashing her wings around an apricot tree.
To see this clearly
is enough.

—*Maya Stein*

CHAPTER FIVE

See More: *Turn Around and Look*

What is art but a way of seeing? —**Thomas Berger**

Clouds #1

I was driving home on I-40, going west.

Tired, needing to just get there, I drove.

As I neared a ridge, I saw clouds coalesce into a most fantastical horse, reared up on his back legs, so realistic (and ominous) that it scared me. *A message of some sort?* I wondered. I looked at cars in the other lane to check their reaction. Nothing. They sped past. I drove on, doing the mental equivalent of the cartoon shaking head, trying to come back to my senses.

And then the horse galloped forward, rearing on its hind legs. At this I pulled to the side of the road and pulled out my camera. I watched for thirty minutes as the horse pranced across the sky, shooting the most amazing cloud formations I have ever seen, all while people sped past going 90 miles per hour, missing the show altogether.

See what's there, not what you expect to see.
Change your perspective—
see from a different angle.
Slow down to see more deeply.
Break apart your vision.

People only see what they are prepared to see. —**Ralph Waldo Emerson**

Clouds #2

Disney World. Speaking at a conference, presidential suite near the Magic Kingdom, at sunset. Amazed that I was so close to the castle in the Magic Kingdom as the sun prepared to set. I watched from one of the many balconies from which I could choose, seeing the sky wane and the castle become an outline. People tiny like little ants swarmed from here to there; lights twinkled on. I watched for quite a while. And when I turned around to head back into my room from the balcony, then—then—I saw the real show, the sunset I had been watching reflected in glory on huge clouds behind me. All I had to do to see it was turn around.

Clouds #3

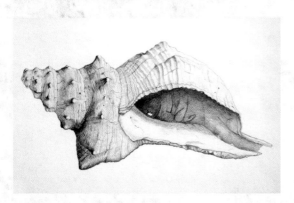

Like most kids, Tess loves to look at clouds. So do I. I fly above them so much, jetting from here to there, and always take pictures. "Oh," my seatmate will inevitably say. "Never flown before?"

"Oh, yes," I say. "I fly nearly every week. I love clouds—aren't they incredible?"

So Tess comes by her fascination easily, I imagine.

She was lying in the hammock with John one afternoon, watching dinosaurs and rabbits float by, and turned her little head toward his. "See the cloud bones?" she said excitedly. "See the cloud bones?"

Clouds #4

When *Life Is a Verb* came out, a high school friend named Keith Bowers surprised me at my first reading in Asheville, where I live. He traveled from our hometown to be there, looking for all the world like he did thirty years ago in high school. I will try not to hate him for that. We've kept in touch since, and he told me one afternoon that the day before his dad died, he asked his dad if he could send a sign from the great beyond. "Yes," his dad said. **"Whenever you see crazy clouds in the sky, you'll know I'm there with you."**

I have looked for crazy clouds every day since. I want to tell my kids the same thing before I die. What a beautiful way to speak up, show up, be seen.

Being creative is, largely, about seeing more. We hear so much about people who have an artist's eye—as if the rest of us don't. We do. We need to use it more.

Drive an Airstream trailer

One eye looks within, the other eye looks without. —**Henri Cartier-Bresson**

I don't long for much.

But I long for an Airstream.

Last year we passed an Airstream dealership on the way home from a training session at my alma mater, Guilford College. "EXIT HERE! EXIT HERE!" I screamed to my business partner, David, who happened to be driving because I was sick with consumption and coughing up a lung.

> [To see far is one thing, going there is another. —**Constantin Brancusi**]

But not coughing so hard I couldn't visit an Airstream dealership. Are you kidding?

David thought I was choking, I had screamed "EXIT HERE" so loudly. After he realized our destination, he no doubt made a mental note to ignore future such outbursts and/or refuse to travel with me when I should by all external measures be hooked up to an iron lung.

Oh, those silver bullets, those containers of the open road. They speak to me. I love their harking to a simpler time, a time when gas was affordable and the open road was open and not clogged with rush-hour traffic. And when I could up and leave at a moment's notice without wondering who would keep watch over ALL. MY. STUFF.

I have not been quiet in my desire for an Airstream. I have had this obsession for a very long time.

My dream is to deck out a big metal vintage tube like a rock band's tour bus. I'll pretend to be Tracy Chapman or Joan Armatrading or Tom Waits or Johnny Cash (pre-posthumously), with 37DAYS or LIFE IS A VERB painted on the side, a little hand-cranked green-and-white awning I could put out when we park, and just flat-out take to the road with Mr. Brilliant, Emma, Tess, and the dawg, Blue (the cats would hate it, trust me), bothering people in independent bookstores across the hills and dales.

Crazy idea? Can I park in your driveway? Do you have an Airstream you're not using anymore? Do you think a teenager, dog, toddler, Mr. Brilliant, and overwrought vegan writer craving Peanut Chews in a small metal tube at 70 miles per hour is a good idea?

It started years ago, this love of Airstreams, and was fueled lately by seeing a revamped Airstream being used as an office. My Lord, what a dream. I can just see traipsing out to the trailer in the driveway in my robe and fuzzy slippers and bed head, much to the dismay of the fancy B&Bs that surround us. I envision myself at a small Formica fold-down table, typing and typing and typing away for hours, sipping Earl Grey lavender tea with soy creamer until I'm completely wired, gnawing on a few radishes, and then folding up my laptop and the table, before the long commute home to make dal and fake-help Emma with her Algebra 2 homework.

I was serious about parking in your driveway.

I fly somewhere almost every week. While I love the patterns of the crops below me as I journey from one place to another, **I long for another perspective, the one at the eye level of corn.** Driving through corn helps us see.

Work called me to Hastings, Nebraska, recently. I would meet amazing people, reconnect with high school and college friends, and eat on a patio in Lincoln the best Indian food I can remember. There is much about that trip that resonated, yes.

A beautiful series of barns. Prairie Loft was the name of the place we would inhabit for two days, engaging teachers and community members in the art of learning. Playing, laughing, learning together. It was magical.

The stark white barns standing against green, green. Barns tall, barns stubby, barns with wooden stalls. A wedding had taken place in the largest of the barns the day before, and magic fairy lights still hung in the rafters where barn swallows dove and lit.

Our barn was open, a rug on the floor to cover the dust, with folding chairs in a circle around it. A long table covered in flowers and beautiful old quilts on one side. Gorgeous vegan food would appear from the simple kitchen made by Lisa and Megan, kitchen goddesses and the hosts of our time there. One morning, we arrived to find them in aprons making homemade pancakes on hot plates in the barn for everyone.

In every group, there is a wisdom that emerges. Sometimes, when the conditions are right (say, when you are in a gorgeous open barn with blue skies and barn swallows swooping past every once in a while and when your belly is full of homemade pancakes cooked in the open air on a small hot plate and covered with jelly somebody canned in their kitchen on the prairie), then there is more wisdom than usual, full rich and filling the crisp air. This was such a time.

And in every group, there are people who speak truth to power and big things can happen. And people who jump in not knowing and not needing to know. And people who sit and resist and finally join. And people for whom the meaning is much, much bigger than what is actually happening in the room. Or barn, for that matter.

And so David and I love this work of unfolding a space for people to wander around in, find meaning in, explore, get hot and messy in, and build relationship in.

The afternoon of our first day, I realized that the old 1940s gorgeously refurbished truck in the parking lot belonged to a man named Jack Sandeen, someone I had immediately been drawn to in the group.

"Jack," I said to him at the break. "That your truck?"

"Yep," he said. "It is. Chevy."

"You think I might stand up on the sideboard runner thing after the session and have somebody take my picture on it?"

"Better," he said. "I'll take you for a ride in it tomorrow."

GET OUT! I was thinking to myself. *REALLY?*

"Thanks, Jack," I said. "I would really love that."

It was a truck the color of butter, all rounded at the edges. The next day, as we approached the afternoon break, Jack motioned for me to come outside with him. "Gonna do better than a ride," he said. "You're gonna drive."

GET OUT! said the yelly voice in my head.

"No, Jack!" I protested. "I couldn't! Just a ride will be great!"

"Nope," he said, handing me the keys. "You're gonna drive. And what's more, you're gonna drive by yourself."

I can't remember being happier or more excited than I was at that moment in that buttercream truck in that sun surrounded by those barns full of those pancakes, holding Jack's keys in my hands. It wasn't just the truck, though that was part of it. It wasn't just the blue sky, though that was part of it. It wasn't just white barns, though that was part of it. It wasn't just the pancakes, though that was part of it, too.

It was that this man entrusted something he clearly loved to a stranger.

I took off down the driveway of the Prairie Loft with country music playing on the radio in the truck, little round dials on the tiny dashboard. The windshield was two tiny panes of glass. I turned on the wipers just to see them work, each coming from the outside of its respective pane to sweep over the tiny expanse of window down and then back out again.

I turned left out of the driveway onto a dirt road, beeped the beepy horn, and waved back to Jack, still watching me go.

Suddenly I was on a long road in sunlight driving down a straight, straight stretch of land surrounded by green corn on either side of it, under a blue sky. Sitting up high in that seat with my hands on the steering wheel, I cried because it was all so, so beautiful.

I mentioned my Airstream dreams to my mother.

"Oh, you always loved Granddaddy's Airstream," she said.

What?

My beloved granddaddy (her father) died when I was only nine.

"Well, at the time he had his stroke and had to live in the rest home, he was living in an Airstream. He made a deal with the rest home that he could park the Airstream in the parking lot so if he ever needed to get away, he could just go out into the parking lot and have his own place. I'm sure you remember seeing it parked there."

All this time, it was a childhood memory, a recognition of deep love—and a knowing—that led to my Airstream love.

As is so often the case, the seed for what we love (and fear) is deep rooted in a past.

Let's go then, you and I, to see.

Sometimes traveling through life quickly—as on an airplane—means that we lose touch with the ground. Knowing what our Airstream is—and why we long for it—helps ground us in our own creativity and movement forward. What is your Airstream? Can you identify why you long for it? Is it something that will help you slow down and see?

give yourself 10

Word: Writer Anton Chekhov said, "I have the feeling that I've seen everything, but failed to notice the elephants." Look around you. What have you failed to notice before right now? Write about it, describe it.

Image: Create an image of what you have just noticed.

give yourself 37

Every day for 37 days, find one thing you have not noticed before and describe it in both words and images. This requires driving the buttercream truck or the Airstream, close to the ground where you can stop, get out, walk around, see at corn level.

ONE LOOKS, LOOKS LONG, AND THE WORLD COMES IN.

—Joseph Campbell

Be the tiny camera

Until I feared I would lose it, I never loved to read. One does not love breathing.
—Harper Lee

A small child in my household, the naming of whom might prove traumatic and so we will simply identify her as being 46 inches tall, months ago dropped my digital camera on the floor. It took some egregious amount of time to find the warranty and drop it off at Best Buy for fixin'.

The part they needed to fix it was back-ordered until April 2050, so Best Buy nicely sent me a new camera without my even asking. I hate to bite a gift horse or whatever that saying is, but I really didn't like the one they sent, so asked pretty please if they could send me a Canon Digital Elph PowerShot SD600 instead, even though it was much more expensive.

Hey, **I've decided that nothing ever comes of not putting stuff out there in the universe, y'know?** The worst they could say—and the most likely reply—was no. They might even go so far as to say, "Hell, no, are you insane?" It was a chance I could live with.

They said yes.

I'm here to tell you that this is a happening little camera. I love everything about it—the shutter delay that plagued me with my old camera is gone, it is fast and small enough to fit into a pocket, the screen is lovely—it's a fine piece of equipment. *I'm very, very happy,* I thought to myself.

I took it on a recent trip and snapped over 366 photographs and a few feature-length documentaries on my one-gigabyte memory card; I couldn't wait to get home and show John the digital trails of my journey.

As I waited for my luggage in New York City near the end of my trip, I saw an elderly man wearing a fabulous anti-racism T-shirt and reached into my bag for my camera. It wasn't there. It was a new bag, so I was sure it was in a new pocket. But as I clawed through the effluvia of my trip—ticket stubs, index cards, fountain pens, Altoids, business cards—my search became more frantic as I realized in one shocking moment that I had left my new, beautiful, wonderful camera on the plane. I felt my throat fill up; I was heartsick. I ran back upstairs and saw one of the flight attendants walking through the terminal. "What gate were we at?" I screamed like a madwoman at her, startling her. "What gate? What gate?" She had no idea who I was. She had never seen me before. I was one of hundreds of passengers she would serve Bloody Mary Mix to that day.

"Um, Gate 22?" she answered.

But I was beyond security; there was no going back. I ran to the Delta counter. The man just shook his head without looking up: "Look, lady, by the time the cleaning crew comes on board, your camera is long gone," he said, returning to his Very Important Paperwork, dismissing me in an instant. There was no plug-in for this kind of loss in his head—it didn't matter to him; I was one of many problems, lost items, complaints that day. I slumped, my head falling down, a tear falling to the floor, then another. It wasn't the camera, although it was a beautiful, fantastical, amazing instrument. It was the pictures.

I had talked legions of important people into making funny faces into the camera so I could send them to cheer my friend and co-teacher, Kichom, in Japan, who couldn't come to the institute this year. Our facial expressions were designed to reflect our shock, horror, and dismay at his absence. I had documented the travels of my gorgeous and rugged Filson luggage that John traded antique maps for at Andy and Lucy's clothing store (bartering is so fantastic—let's all do more of it, okay?). I had photographed all the food that David and Lora forced me to eat at their house in Seattle. I had captured the images of the people in the class I taught, the wonderful French man who makes cheese in Seattle and sells it at the farmers' market, the young toddler in swimming goggles watching musicians at the farmers' market, and amazing zinnias. All gone. All gone. All gone.

In that moment, hot tears in my eyes, slumped over the Delta counter, I realized that an essay I had recently written about "Buddhist Economics" had been about the elimination of craving: "While the materialist is mainly interested in goods, the Buddhist is mainly interested in liberation . . . **It is not wealth that stands in the way of liberation, but the attachment to wealth**; not the enjoyment of pleasurable things, but the craving for them."

The universe gives us lessons, doesn't it? Here was mine. I needed to give up my craving for that camera and those images, didn't I?

When John and I were first together as a couple, we went to Santa Fe. I realized as I looked at jewelry during that trip that I had never bought myself any jewelry as an adult: in fact, I didn't wear any jewelry or adornment of any kind. For many reasons, I needed to mark this new era in my life and did so with a remarkable silver ring that I wore every day, a ring with sugilite and turquoise and lapis, a gorgeous architecture of power, independence, trueness. It was a symbol far more than it was a ring.

A few years later I gave a speech in DC, where we then lived. When I got home, I looked down at my right hand and realized in horror that the central stone in that ring—a beautiful, deep purple sugilite—was gone. Numb with sick, I called the hotel to ask if anyone had found it; of course, they hadn't. I knew they wouldn't. It was one of a thousand lost things, wasn't it? None of which meant anything to them, but everything to me. I had a moment's horror, that heart kind—the sinking-pit feeling, the rising heat, the bile, the hot face, the stinging tears. And then, a moment later as I looked down at my hand, now a gaping hole where that lovely stone once rested, I realized with a quiet peace that I had internalized the ring, that the meaning of it was now in me, not out there on my finger, and that I was peaceful with not having, that "having had" was enough, that I felt strong on my own now, the talisman having served its purpose until I could myself be strong.

I wrapped the gaping ring in tissue and put it away. Very soon even the pentimento of its structure had disappeared from my finger. A few years later when the opportunity arose for a trip to Santa Fe, I slipped it into my luggage—perhaps that little shop would still be there. It was. As I entered, I told the salesclerk about getting the ring there many years earlier, about losing the stone, about what it meant to me. I unwrapped it and held it in front of her like an offering. I thought I heard a small gasp. "Wait here," she said quietly. "Wait right here. I'll be right back."

She was back in an instant, trailed by a beautiful man with a gray ponytail and a smile like people smile in Santa Fe, that happy, fulfilled, *I'm living my dream in an amazing place and I'm an artist* kind of smile. I held out the ring to

If I could do what I want with my eyes alone, I would be happy. —Richard Avedon

him and that happy smile burst into sunshine. "Oh, my," he said. "Oh, my. I haven't seen this ring in years and years. It's like seeing an old friend again."

He sat down slowly.

"He made this ring," the shop clerk explained as he held the ring and turned it in his hands, touching it quietly and smiling. "He made it and it was the only one like it that he made. I recognized it immediately when you unwrapped it and it just so happened that he was in the shop today. I knew he would be thrilled to see it again."

Mr. Ring Maker and I talked for quite some time in that small, crowded shop, me telling him the story of how I came to love and own the ring, what it meant to me then and what it means to me now. He held it lovingly and promised to shine it and replace the sugilite for me, then ship it home to me. I wear it every day now, too, not because I need it for strength, but because I once did.

Julio Lopez at the Delta ticket counter in New York's JFK airport just couldn't bear what he saw—a gray-haired, tired, slightly rumpled woman who had been traveling for twelve days and was quietly crying at the Delta counter as if she couldn't believe what she had done, having been summarily dismissed by his co-worker. "Let me run to Gate 22," he said to me. "I'll do my best."

He was gone a long time.

I gave up hope. I knew I would leave without it. And I also realized that it was okay, that the images were really inside me, that I could be okay with the loss. I made my peace with it, standing there near Mr. Dismissive Man.

The irony of the moment wasn't lost on me—do we write about and teach about what we most need to learn?

Just then Mr. Julio Lopez came bounding toward me. Suddenly, from quite a distance, he held up a small red camera bag in his hand, triumphant at finding it on board that plane!

(If you fly through JFK and see Julio Lopez at the Delta counter, give him a hug for me. My only regret in the excitement and relief of the moment is that I didn't take his picture.)

Not having and then having again—I've roads to go down yet in my extraction from craving, but it was a good lesson, a message, a sign that I could do it.

Listen to the messages you're being given. The universe is speaking to us—what is it saying? Why aren't we listening? Be the tiny camera. Sometimes we need external symbols of worth, strength, happiness—the ring, the photos: What is it for you, I wonder? Hold them tight, those symbols, and be prepared to let them fly away, too. Don't rely on them too, too much. Become them, internalize them, live them. Even give them away. They will have more power that way.

give yourself 10

Word: What are you attached to? My friend Jodi told of a colleague having GPS at the Grand Canyon to tell him where he was. "You're right here," Jodi responded. Write about what helps you see, what keeps you from seeing, what helps you remember or capture the essence of an experience.

Image: Look up and find the beauty that's in front of you—every object is filled with a story. A vase, a sunrise, a story—draw the object you see first on your desk or in your room when you read this.

give yourself 37

Look for beauty. And where you feel compelled to remember experiences by buying mementos, restrain. Instead, seek to internalize the beauty of the moments you want to remember so they are a part of you, not an add-on to you.

RE-INVESTING IN ONE'S OWN LITTLE MOMENTS OF INSIGHT IS VERY IMPORTANT.

—Anish Kapoor

Eat on a lake

A lake is the landscape's most beautiful and expressive feature. It is earth's eye;
looking into which the beholder measures the depth of his own nature.

—Henry David Thoreau

"Let's grab a cup of coffee sometime soon," I e-mailed.

"Sounds good," Brooks e-mailed back. "It's supposed to be a beautiful day on Wednesday—how about going out on Beaver Lake?"

I hesitated.

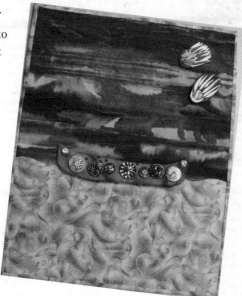

Should I tell him that the last time I got in a boat, I single-handedly capsized it, with everyone aboard joining me in the water, people who—it appears—had no sense of humor, of adventure, of *joie de vivre*, people who worried about their hairdos and boating shoes? And who knew that you need to step into the middle of the boat? Is there a School for Common Sense that I somehow missed? Was I absent that day in class? Is that the day I had my wisdom teeth cut out and drank Skippy peanut butter milk shakes until I was Skippied out forever?

"That'd be great!" I said. "I love boats!"

I should have known better than think I could fool a longtime sailing man like Brooks. He's spent his life on boats, designing his first one when he was nine, building it when he was eleven, launching it on his twelfth birthday.

I was wallpapering my room with *Tiger Beat* posters of Bobby Sherman, chasing Bryan Stephens, playing Pee Wee football, wearing Peter Max hot pants, and selling and eating obscene numbers of Girl Scout cookies (Thin Mints rule!) when I was twelve, not building a boat.

It was a beautiful, blue sky, cloudless, clear see-forever kind of day. I met Brooks at Beaver Lake.

"Since we'll be sitting at opposite ends of the boat," he said when I arrived, "I brought breakfast in separate bags for us."

I looked down. In two canvas bags were identical, beautiful little offerings:

a tall, silver cylinder thermos of Counter Culture coffee, hot, black, strong, like I like it. With them were muffins, napkins, and a bottle of orange juice wrapped in a towel for each of us, like a prize. It was like going to camp and having Mama pack my favorite cookies in the pocket of one of her aprons.

I decided right then and there that I was going to eat breakfast in a boat on Beaver Lake every day for the rest of my life.

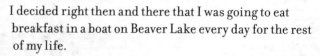

"Your boat is beautiful," I said, looking down at a dark blue Adirondack guideboat trimmed in cherry, with caned seats, long oars that crossed over each other when you pulled, one hand on top of the other, effortlessly, or so it would seem. I was Kate Hepburn in *The African Queen* if, in fact, she was packing a cell phone and a bottle of Brita-filtered tap water for the trip.

Brooks slid the boat into the water, then got in. Effortlessly. Like he had been doing it since he was— oh, say—nine years old.

I stood, paralyzed on the dock. I'd estimate the water was only a few feet deep there, so it wasn't the fear of drowning that stopped me. It was the memory of that capsized boat; it was a lack of surety. "Where should I step?" I asked.

Brooks smiled and said something about the middle of the boat.

With that, I stepped in with my left foot, into the center, leaving my right foot on the pier for the moment, and holding on to whatever that thing is called that sticks up from the pier. Suddenly the boat started moving out from the pier, taking my left leg with it while my right one stayed solidly on the pier, creating in mere seconds an increasingly dire situation in which I was soon to be: (1) split in half, (2) in the water, (3) in the water with Brooks, organic spelt muffins, orange juice, and two thermoses of black coffee.

I pawed at the boat with my left leg, like a small impotent palsy, trying to get it to move back to the right toward the pier. Brooks subtly helped—and without laughing, for which I give him Big Credit.

It only lasted a few seconds, and then we were on our way. But my Lord, the boat was so deep into the water that I felt like we'd pitch over at any moment, or the water would start streaming in over the sides like those endless pools you see at the homes of movie stars where the pool seems to go over the horizon into the ocean (since they're inevitably living in Malibu). It is a boat meant for slicing through water, a low profile, deep deep into the lake.

So there I sat in my pullover shirt and pinchy approximation of boating clothing, not moving a muscle.

"If you want to try to row the thing," Brooks had written before we went, "don't wear a buttondown shirt. Wear a pullover one instead."

I pondered the physics of that statement for quite a while, sitting in front of my computer screen. What on earth was the reason for that? I wondered. Is it possible that the glinting of sunlight on buttons might blind the beavers? Are there killer fish in Beaver Lake hell-bent on enlarging their button collection? Finally the suspense was too much for me, and I e-mailed Brooks back to ask.

"The handle of the right oar catches in the front of men's button shirts. For women it's generally the left oar. You can wear a button shirt and row with long oars safely if you leave the shirt unbuttoned. Or you can row okay in a buttoned shirt with short oars but I don't have any of those."

There are so very many things I don't know.

As we swept into water, it occurred to me that any American literature major worth their salt is in love with *Moby-Dick,* this one no exception to that rule. Herman Melville would have to love water to write such a tale, though all through the writing he was either digging in the basement or sitting in that small upstairs room at Arrowhead in Pittsfield, Massachusetts, looking at a hump of a mountain, Mount Greylock, that inspired the whale.

> THE ARTIST AND THE PHOTOGRAPHER SEEK THE MYSTERIES AND THE ADVENTURE OF EXPERIENCE IN NATURE.
>
> —Ansel Adams

He did love water: "Take almost any path you please," he wrote in *Moby-Dick* in 1851, "and ten to one it carries you down in a dale, and leaves you there by a pool in the stream. **There is magic in it.** Let the most absent-minded of men be plunged in his deepest reveries—stand that man on his legs, set his feet a-going, and he will infallibly lead you to water, if water there be in all that region. Should you ever be athirst in the great American desert, try this experiment, if your caravan happen to be supplied with a metaphysical professor. Yes, as every one knows, meditation and water are wedded forever."

There are different forms to meditation, I realized that morning on the lake. Some involve whale-shaped mountains, some involve journeys to high altitudes, some entail absolute silence or require renunciation, and at least one of them involves long oars, black coffee, and buttonless shirts.

I'm a redhead. Well, a former redhead, now white-headed, but with the skin of a redhead still, complete with memories of long-sleeved white shirts on the beach and zinc oxide under a plastic triangle that hung, impotently, from my significant cat-eye glasses as a child. Pretty picture, I know. That's all to say that SPF 400 sunscreen doesn't suffice. So as I settled in, I pulled on my new Tilley Raffia crushable and breathable hat, the one with the highest ultraviolet protection rating of UPF 50+ to block 98 percent of harmful UVA and UVB rays, backed by a two-year all-perils insurance policy against loss and a Velcro-sealed secret pocket to hold valuables—the first hat that has ever fit my considerably sized head—and we boated, the only vessel on the lake.

Brooks sliced long oars through water, one hand over top of the other, as I centered my body weight nonchalantly, but with intention.

We visited a large, industrious, impressive beaver dam. "Damn," I said, trailing my hand beside the boat in the water, like all those women do in movies. "Those beavers are busy."

"Hence the name," said Brooks in response, smiling as he rowed.

And so, my breakfast journey on Beaver Lake brought me five simple messages:

1. **Always say yes to a boat trip.** Don't let overturned boats in your past dictate future adventures.

2. When surrounded by water, it might be a good idea to **step into the center** of what can carry you through it. Don't hesitate, or the boat will move away from the pier and you'll fall in the gap.

3. **Wear a pullover shirt.** Always be prepared for rowing; dress for it, in fact, whether you know if you'll row or not. **Don't let buttons stand in your way.**

4. **Whenever possible, eat breakfast on a lake.** On Beaver Lake. In an Adirondack guideboat. With a friend who knows how to pack a breakfast, how to row, and how to tell a story.

5. Get as close as you can to the water. **Look beneath its surface.** You might find yourself there, in someone else's story. Just maybe. And even if not, you'll see the reflection of some pretty spectacular clouds.

"A lake," wrote William Wordsworth, **"carries you into recesses of feeling otherwise impenetrable."** The surface of that water, dipped into. The image of ourselves in waves, mirrors. Ourselves reflected in something with immeasurable depth. There is magic in it, yes, Mr. Melville. I came home that very morning and cleaned off our canoe. John and I are going boating. Seek to place yourself firmly in the landscape.

give yourself 10

Word: Describe yourself as part of the landscape rather than separate from it. Look out your window and place yourself deep into the grass or water or sky. What do you see?

Image: What kind of landscape are you a part of? Desert? Mountain? Waterside? Nature/landscape/wisdom sits in places. Pull your camera back and see yourself in the landscape; create the sense of that "belonging" in image form.

give yourself 37

Do things that aren't comfortable for you—walk toward the fear that you might overturn the boat. Put yourself in situations out in nature that make you pay attention to what is around you: Walk on a brick wall in the park and feel the heightened sensation of nearly falling, of needing to balance. Each day, balance in such a way between comfort and fear. Each day, lie down in the grass.

In nature there are few sharp lines. —A. R. Ammons

Listen to tiny fishies

Contemplation is the root of awareness and creativity. —**Sandra Chantry**

I'm curious about Bose QuietComfort Acoustic Noise Canceling Headphones.

My life and jobs have taken me to more than sixty countries, some just for a few days; others, like Sri Lanka and Germany, for many months. I've been privileged to bump up against some of this planet's amazing humans and our diverse ways of being in the world, allowed to see firsthand the tip of the culture iceberg and sometimes at least small glimpses into that deeper, darker

part below the waterline—the part that can get dangerous if you don't know it's there—enlarging with frequent flier miles the worldview that began in a small southern town with one movie theater, one barbershop (my daddy's), and hardly any Catholics.

So I've measured out my life not in coffee spoons, but in Boeing seats, a long line of 9As and 17Cs (anything but middles!), winging from port to port in unnatural seated positions with nothing but air and hope beneath me, important in my power suit once landed, leading a board of directors from one bilateral meeting to another while they complained about Spanish restaurants not opening until 9:00 p.m. (those late-eating European heathens!), staying in Frank Lloyd Wright's Imperial Hotel in Tokyo where their complaints centered on room size (imagine the nerve of Mr. Wright being culturally alert!), circumnavigating the globe on a ship for four months, watching the new year arrive over Sydney harbor, speaking at a South African conference just after Mandela was elected, sampling pepper vodka in an amazing Russian restaurant in Helsinki, seeing Picasso's *Guernica* in Spain, and standing in front of all the pieces of my favorite—Paolo Uccello's *Battle of San Romano*—in Florence, Paris, and London, spread as it is around the world. (Uccello, by the way, was the son of a barber; perhaps that explains the connection I feel to him. Or maybe it was those wacky polyhedral hats.)

All those meanderings were true gifts, a visceral reminder of the same and not same, the known and not known, the understood and not understood, and the feared and not feared on this planet of ours.

And so I lived at 37,000 feet with a seat belt fastened low and tight across my lap for years, crisscrossing the globe like one of those maps with red tacks and skinny threads in a War Room or on that nice television show *CSI,* where they're forever tracking a serial killer who strikes at consistent distances between subway stops and pretzel stands, creating lines of connection that still remain, quiet sometimes and then emerging, friends around the world.

In the fall of 1995, I returned after three weeks abroad, an exhausting but satisfying trip, resulting in Successful and Of Course Important Business Stuff and, more important, meeting a wise and funny man named Eliav, a former Israeli tank commander who writes about leadership issues and who always makes me both think and laugh, an undeniably fantastic combination in any language.

On Sunday morning after I arrived, my daughter Emma—then three years old—snuggled into bed to welcome me home with laughter, shrieking, tickling happiness. And then she spoke, holding my face in her hands: "Mama," she said quietly. "I had a lot of dreams while you were gone."

"What'd you dream about, Peanut?" I said, hardly stopping for the answer as I prepared to swoop her up and make chocolate chip pancakes, the batter a simple delivery device for the cocoa.

"I dreamed I was a little tiny fish in a big, big ocean, and I couldn't find my mommy."

( ). ◄——— That's a picture of my stunned silence, as I looked at John from across the bed. **I had finally stopped flying long enough to hear her.** She stopped me cold.

Yes. Well. It was a clear message. A message that comes along once—a message that begs to be listened to, one where you hope the noise around it is reduced enough so you can actually hear the real part, the part you should hear and heed and do something about, the part where you need the noise of airplane engines to stop so they won't keep the message from emerging. That's what got me thinking about those Bose QuietComfort Acoustic Noise Canceling Headphones.

[
To look is to learn,
if you listen carefully.
—Per Arnold
]

Sometimes I need the quiet they would provide, without the cutting-me-off-from-others part I see so much, that inalienable sanctity that is created, a bubble of solitude in which not only do you stop the noise, but you also stop the singing, the connection, the dialogue.

There's so much noise in the world, isn't there? So much more than those summers when I played outside in the creek all day, coming home only when I heard my father whistle for dinnertime. Now constant noise, warnings, static surround me—in the Atlanta airport last Wednesday, television sets blared with nothing but bad news, loud-voiced people shouted instructions about boarding by zone, and, yes, of course—I was surrounded by Ubiquitous Cell Phone Conversations that all begin with a kind of Global Positioning Announcement, placing Self in Universe in Time: "Yes, I'm at the gate now," "We just landed!" "I'm walking toward baggage claim," "It's ten o'clock here!" or my personal favorite, "I'm in the bathroom; hold on a minute." (Really, must I participate in their every movement? Pun intended.)

Emma's tiny fish dream was a message I listened to: I left my job a few months afterward. As much as I enjoyed the work, there was no contest. She was my life, not business meetings with people I would never see again; not platinum Delta cards that like a lottery just provide me an opportunity to compete more effectively to sit in nicer chairs periodically; not a passport that served as a brag book, a talisman of importance; and not all the fancy restaurants and hotels in the world. This little human needed me to be here to laugh with her and kiss her boo-boos and teach her how to tie her little tiny shoes, not collect countries like so many notches on my bedpost.

And so I finally heard her little three-year-old wisdom.

What does it mean to really listen to the messages that are all around us, the things that do—indeed—come from the mouths of babes? Where there are migraines, there's a message, isn't there? Where there is fatigue, a message is desperately trying to escape. Where there is dread, there's a story. What does it mean to really hear, to reduce the noise to its most important elements, to stop long enough to hear beyond or inside the static, that busyness, all that damn communication? How hard it is to hear the things we really need to hear.

If life is too noisy and it's headphones I seek—even metaphorically—at what point am I escaping the noise by disconnecting altogether?

When I turn on my microwave, the radio that sits near it becomes full of static, making it hard to hear those nice people on NPR. When I pretend to listen to someone while checking my e-mail or when I ask a question without waiting for the answer or deflecting the answers I don't want to hear, the same thing happens: static, dispersion of attention, a reduction of the teller and the listener, both.

John was once called to appraise the library of a pediatrician who had practiced for fifty years. Alzheimer's was capturing the doctor's mind, and his family wanted to take care of his library before he slipped into deeper fog. As John asked questions of him, this straight, tall, patrician physician kept wondering whether the books were his golf clubs.

Undaunted, John continued: "Tell me, Doctor, after working with children for fifty years, what's your biggest lesson about kids?"

Suddenly the doctor snapped to attention, emerging from the dusk of disease to answer with great clarity: **"Never, never interrupt a child when a child is speaking to you."** And with that, he was back to his golf clubs.

Never interrupt. You want to hear what they really want to say, to go where they want to take you, not where you want to go, to move at their speed, not yours, to hear those little fishies when they're telling you something important—children or adults alike.

And now I've got another small fishie in the house. Tess is six now. But I've learned, haven't I? I really took Emma's tiny fish message to heart and changed my life. Didn't I?

Tess speaks in full paragraphs after starting with one-word phrases ("Peace!" with two outstretched fingers was one of her first, my little hippie baby), then two-word declarations ("MY bottle!"). Pseudo-sentences followed ("Daddy on a bike!" was her first, documenting that momentous occasion when she saw John magically floating toward her on an object that others called a bike). She's deep into complicated paragraphs now, intricate tales about ducks and horses and fire trucks and delicious Popsicles that inevitably all begin the same way: "One day . . ."

One of her very first phrases?

"Mama on a plane!"

Perhaps I've got more work to do.

Remember that tiny fish in a big, big ocean. Find a way to hear what it's saying to you. Identify the spam in your life. Like everything else, it's a metaphor—it is noise, distraction, static that's filling up the spaces. What's the static that prevents me from hearing myself, that spam that clutters up the spaciousness that I need in order to create?

give yourself 10

Word: List the spam in your life. Part of the creative spirit is to create spaciousness to create. What spam can you let go of? Do you get endless numbers of online e-zines? Unsubscribe. Most of them are just telling you what you need to learn (from them, no doubt).

Image: What does listening look like? Create an image of listening. (And, perhaps, of what spam keeps you from fully hearing.)

give yourself 37

For 37 days, for one hour each day, just do one thing at a time—if you're eating, turn off your computer. If you're writing, don't drink coffee. Eliminate all distractions just for one hour a day. Write about what you notice when you eliminate distractions from the one task at hand. What does it look or feel like to listen to yourself instead of listening to others?

THE MAN INCAPABLE OF CONTEMPLATION
CANNOT BE AN ARTIST, BUT ONLY A
SKILLFUL WORKMAN.

—Ananda Coomaraswamy

Keep on looking up

The true harvest of my life is intangible—a little star dust caught, a portion of the rainbow I have clutched. —**Henry David Thoreau**

I taught a Junior Achievement class for nine weeks at a local high school one fall—the focus was jobs and careers after high school, that ubiquitous school-to-work transition we all adore, that move into responsible adulthood we so longed for as a kid, only now realizing the error of our ways.

The eleventh-grade English class that I invaded was in the high school that my older daughter, Emma, would attend beginning the next fall. In the spirit of full disclosure, let me just say that I volunteered primarily so I could live out my lifelong dream to be an Industrial Spy, checking out the school before Emma hit the hallways. And of course, I also wanted to wow the kids in the class, get them talking about ethical dilemmas in the workplace, give them some case studies to chew on. I imagined we would have fascinating conversations about the nature of work, finding meaning and passion in our careers, helping others, yada, yada, yada. You get the picture.

I think it's fair to say that I was a tad bit naive about how a high school classroom operates.

They were underwowed. And even that is an understatement.

I've spent the last twenty years as a speaker and trainer; nothing prepared me for the challenges of those twenty-six human beings. Even more than the way the kids hit the floor when a car backfired outside and even more than the difficulty I had in even getting them to stop talking or wake up long enough to hear my glorious outpourings of irrelevant wisdom—what most impressed itself on my little noggin during that experience was the smallness of the dreams those young adults had for their lives—they didn't see a big future ahead of them. The one young woman with some serious spunk and a spark in her eye missed the last four sessions; she had been expelled for fighting.

Some of those young adults, in fact, saw no future at all for themselves—they didn't have an expansive view of what could be. I found that sad; no, it was more than sad. It was disheartening and terrible and avoidable and awful and more. I organized a career fair there the next spring to provide them with some options. I wanted them to dream big; at the very least, I wanted to dream big around them, in their general proximity, in hopes that some of that optimism and hope and just plain caring would rub off.

For years, Emma said she wanted to be an astronomer. Even when she veered to veterinarian, meteorologist, equestrian athlete, manga illustrator, or professional tuba player, she always came back to the skies. It is fitting, that choice. After all, it was the sale of John's antique Brashear telescope that funded her birth, insurance not being what it used to be. When she was little, she pronounced that the stars were "very messy."

Emma has a dog-eared boxed set of the video series *The Astronomers*, which we have watched no fewer than 413 times. At an age when girls fall away from the sciences in large numbers under the weight of societal messages that they "don't do math and science," I was determined to support her interests, no matter her final decisions about what she will study and do and be when she grows up.

The summers bring out my best Googling skills as I hunt for interesting activities for me and the kids to do. Once it was sewing class (Emma used to design her own character dolls from anime films), and one week I discovered that several distinguished astronomers were going to be guest lecturers at a high school summer camp held at the Pisgah Astronomical Research Institute about an hour-and-a-half drive from where we live. It was too late to register Emma for the two-week camp, but after I described her astronomical interests, the director graciously invited us to attend any of the guest lectures we'd like, from 1:00 to 2:00 p.m. each day. Emma perused the choices, selecting two: "Observational Astronomy Challenges in Detecting Low Mass Stellar Companions" (huh?) and "Extrasolar Planets: A First Reconnaissance" (huh?). "These look fantastic!" she squealed. "Indeed!" I said, wondering if she had been switched at birth.

The first lecture was given by Dr. Mercedes Lopez-Morales, a small woman with a big mind. We were treated royally by the organizers, each taking great care in introducing Emma to the guest speakers and staff. In the midst of all that was happening, Dr. Lopez-Morales sat and talked quietly with Emma, asking about her interests in astronomy and telling about her own education to give Emma a picture of how it happened for her. In her quiet way, I could tell that Emma was excited, nervous, awed. Another man joined in the conversation, a big man in a Hawaiian-print shirt and khaki shorts who had an easy laugh. He not only encouraged Emma to continue pursuing her love of astronomy, but talked with her about playing the tuba. "As a tuba player, you'd be a fantastic didjeridou player!" he exclaimed with the excitement of a child. The didjeridou, it appears, is his instrument of choice. We just happened to have a didjeridou lying about the house from a trip I took to Australia, so she was excited to try out his theory. "He was really nice," she said on the way home.

We drove back there on Thursday to hear one of the most famous astronomers living today—Dr. Paul Butler. Dr. Butler has been on the front pages of major newspapers the world over, has discovered gazillions of new extrasolar planets (or perhaps it was fewer than a gazillion, I'm not sure), and was named one of *Time* magazine's hundred most influential people for the twenty-first century. He is, as we say in the vernacular, a Very Big Deal. We were excited to meet him.

Turns out, he was the energetic didjeridou player who had struck up a conversation with Emma the day before.

Here's a man who is not only brilliant and passionate about his work, but who has a real talent for encouraging young people, engaging them, and explaining tough subjects in understandable terms. (I'm pleased to report that I was able to follow his talk almost completely except for one teeny part about sumpin-sumpin I couldn't pronounce.)

When he finished his talk, we went to the front to thank him. Emma was too shy to ask for his autograph, but John asked for her as she stood shyly back. "I'd be delighted to," he answered. "Emma, how do you spell your name?" he asked, making a special effort to bring her into the conversation. She stepped forward and talked with him. On a small poster of his extrasolar planet research, Dr. Butler wrote something that will come to mean more and more to Emma as she grows: "To Emma, Keep looking up! R. Paul Butler."

What great advice.

Oprah once did a series of shows in which she granted the "wildest dreams" of women from her audience. At the end of the series, she quietly said that what struck her most about the whole process was how small those wildest dreams were—**we need to dream bigger for ourselves,** she said. I wonder why we settle for less than star dust. Is it that we believe ourselves not worthy? Are we afraid of falling from such a great height? Don't we know that the universe will catch us? Can't we see that the view on the way down will be spectacular? What are your biggest creative dreams, I wonder.

Keep looking up, wherever "up" is to you.

(And while you're at it, look for ways to help teenagers keep looking up, too. They need us to peel back the clouds and enlarge the night sky for them.)

give yourself 10

Word: Describe yourself at your most potent, happy, fulfilled creative self. Your most magnificent self. Dream, dream big, dream in Technicolor—on a huge canvas—like the night sky.

Image: What does your galaxy look like?

give yourself 37

I wonder as I ponder Emma's trajectory: What rainbow have I clutched? And you? Have you been too earthbound, too small, too contained in your wildest dreams? Discover the ways you limit your canvas. What are the ways you make your canvas small or minimize your palette? Stretch your canvas— identify the dreams and look for ways you can engage them each day for 37 days.

Look in the square

The eyes are not responsible when the mind does the seeing. —**Publilius Syrus**

When I was in junior high and high school, I was an artist, taking drawing and painting classes and expecting my parents to hang my oversize and pensive and hormonal portraits of monarch butterflies over the fireplace, that place of honor. They did.

At that age, I was a taller version of the small child who makes a "stained glass" vase from an Ivory dish-soap bottle in pre-K and a balloon papier-mâché bowl with painted yarn in bad colors and awkward scrolls in Vacation Bible School, proudly presenting the treasure, noticing whether or not it was displayed afterward in the TV room.

Perhaps I am still an artist—aren't we all?—but life pushes it out of us. As Picasso said, "All children are artists. The problem is how to remain an artist once we grow up."

My digital camera is broken, having died a Terrible and Tragic Death at the Hands of a Child Who Shall Not be Named, but who is 4 feet tall and whose initials include a *T*. That's all to say that I'd love to illustrate this story with the pencil drawings around which it circles, but can't at the moment. So imagine, if you will, two pencil drawings, one of an old man in a weathered hat, standing with his arms hanging limply by his sides and looking straight into your gaze. The other is a woman also staring straight ahead, but sitting, her hands gathered in her lap. They are big drawings, framed in wood from my uncle's old homestead, a satisfying gray wood, weathered by the years, the sun, the rain. He gathered the wood when the house came down, crafting frames for these drawings from the timbers, a surprise for me.

These many years later my daughter Emma is a cartoonist; her drawings (okay, I'm biased, but surely this is close to the Objective Truth) are fantastic feats of cartooning. She has a well-honed sense of gesture, of tone, of movement, of glance and humor—she can even do hands!—and this week, she has ventured out from the cartoon world to drawing from life, a pencil portrait of her friend Brittany one of her first works.

She was disappointed by her effort.

I tried to reassure her in a way that might not have been all that reassuring, really: "It's tough drawing people from life—I'm no good at it, but you have great potential."

"But, Mom," she protested, "those pictures you did of the old man and woman hanging in Grammy's kitchen are amazing."

I WRITE ENTIRELY TO FIND OUT WHAT I'M THINKING, WHAT I'M LOOKING AT, WHAT I SEE AND WHAT IT MEANS. WHAT I WANT AND WHAT I FEAR.

—Joan Didion

But I didn't draw them from life like you did, I said. I drew a matrix of 1-inch by 1-inch squares on photographs of those two people. Then I drew a matrix of the same number of squares on the drawing paper. And then I drew what I saw in each square, not a nose, but abstract lines in a box. Not an eye, but solid moments of dark against sharp whites, dots of gray on islands of black. And in such a way I drew those people—freed up from my belief that lips are too hard to draw, freed up from my perception of "lip-ness."

While mine was a simpler process than Emma's—and perhaps not as sophisticated—it occurred to me that other, more complex, parts of life could benefit from the same approach.

What would happen in my daily life if I divorced the lifetime of history I have with the thing in front of me—the object, the situation, the person, the opportunity—and simply looked at the components of the thing instead, the discrete pieces that make it up, the 1-inch squares of lines and shadows, not my expectations that they will form a lip, an eye, a nose? **What if I divorced my perception of it from the thing itself, if I stopped seeing what I expect to see and saw what I really see?** As my friend David wrote to me in an e-mail recently:

Seeing is not as easy as it might seem. Visual artists train for years to see what is there, not what they think is there. Seeing requires a return to the time before you had words, concepts, and definitions for everything. You'd be amazed at how many colors there are in a "yellow" #2 pencil when you look past the idea of "yellow pencil" and actually see the shapes, shadows, and light.

Seeing. We are trained for dullness, David says. Yes, we've lost the skill of seeing, we've begun clinging to the beliefs we have about the way things are, building life rafts of "pencil," the idea, not the thing in front of us, not really.

David Hockney's hundreds of Polaroids create layers of meaning and angles of vision (okay, I'll mention him, but I'm still miffed with him over his theory on the use of optical devices by old masters); Chuck Close's squares connect pure color into meaning (I think perhaps he stole the idea from me; I'm considering suing). What are we made up of, if not these small squares of color, tone, story, meaning?

What if I looked past the idea of "criminal" or "gang member" or "homeless person" or "alcoholic" or "teenager" or "CEO" and actually saw the shapes, shadows, and light that make up those people? Would that change the picture I draw of them inside my head and the one I act on outside of my head? Would it involve stepping back from my reductive story of them to see all the hues and colors that make them up, all the stories that have created meaning in their lives, all the ways in which they have become the people who stand in front of me? Would it mean that I need to grant them the same level of specificity that I grant myself? That I need to change my perspective in order to see them, just as I do when I see a self-portrait by Chuck Close?

THERE ONCE WAS AN OWL WHO SAT IN AN OAK, THE MORE IT HEARD, THE LESS IT SPOKE . . . THE LESS IT SPOKE, THE MORE IT HEARD.

—Gentlehawk

What picture would I create of others if I really looked at what was there, not what I imagined was there; if I really saw the shapes and shadows of their lives and not my interpretation of them?

As Thoreau has said, the question is not what you look at, but what you see.

Teilhard de Chardin said that "the whole of life lies in the verb *seeing*." See again. See what is, not what you believe. See what is, not what you expect to see. See what is, not what you have named in your own mind. Go back to a time before you had words, concepts, and definitions for everything, when the possibility of a person, an object, a situation was unlimited, full of shapes and colors and a meaning all its own.

Just see.

give yourself 10

Word: What one impossible or overwhelming challenge are you facing? Just as a trip to Russia begins with booking an airline ticket, so, too, your challenge begins with one step. Write about what emerges from you as your first true step.

Image: Draw an image that represents your challenge. Then lightly draw 1-inch blocks on the surface of the image. Using the technique I used in this story (drawing a "map" of 1-inch blocks on an image), "draw" your challenge in discrete steps, one piece per box onto another index card.

give yourself 37

Create a 1-inch square every day on the back of an index card. Using crayons, color the square solid to match the "feel" and "mood" of that day. In such a way, you create an aggregate "quilt" of moods. Life is incremental like that.

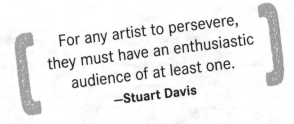

For any artist to persevere, they must have an enthusiastic audience of at least one.
—**Stuart Davis**

CHAPTER SIX

Get Present: *Show Up Like Magic*

*There are moments when you absolutely need someone to show up like magic,
not because you need something nice, but because you need your world view
transformed. You need some hope to be born in you. You need to know in one moment
that someone believes in you. You need a kindness midwife to hold the space so you
can show up like magic for someone else the next time around . . .* —**Jen Lemen**

When my friend Gay tells a story, it comes
out like a hot knife through rich butter—all
soft, fluid, full, with a drawl that makes
you want to move to Mississippi and listen
to a big bearded man in a scratchy green
sweater read Faulkner out loud to you in
a hot room where dust motes float heavy
in the air when the faded velvet curtains
dare to part ever so slightly against the hot
white day.

stop resisting.
Create magic for someone else.
Lighten your spirit.
Follow the thread.
Make strong offers.

That's just to say that the woman can tell a
story.

And here's a childhood remembering of
hers that left an image I won't soon forget. It is a remembering about being
fully present in the back of a hot car on a long trip, legs stuck to the plastic
seat covers—and about creating the glorious spaciousness that is needed for
that kind of awareness.

Like many of us of a certain age, her family went on summertime road trips,
a special kind of Interstate Hell for parents with small children, I now know.

How amazing it is that year after year in the middle of the night so many parents of (supposedly) sound mind actually place their children in the backseat to embark on long, un-air-conditioned summer journeys, drawing an imaginary line down the center of the seat to keep us kids from looking at each other (glances can only escalate to pinching and sibling torture of kinds too numerous and just plain awful to elucidate), threatening us with creamed corn and sauerkraut with weenies for dinner if we crossed the line, and motoring their way to Vacation Land, a place that, no matter when we asked, was always just 10 more miles.

In the back of that 1956 Chevy (insert your own make and model here), Gay recalled hot summer days of driving on the open road, thighs sticking to car seats, her arm held out the window, catching and riding the wind, up and down, quietly flying there in the backseat, unnoticed, hot and cool air catching her arm and making it float up, then down.

As they rode mile after mile, Gay said, she would divest herself of pieces of clothing and belongings, first taking off one white sock, then the other, her hat, one small shoe and then the other, her small baby doll's special Easter dress and bonnet, the doll itself, holding each one out the window for an almost interminable time, feeling the wind resistance, the aerodynamic thrust of the object, its fluttering in the breeze. She would hold it, hold it, hold it, and then—without a sound—her fingers would quickly stretch straight out and the sock or the doll dress or the hat would simply fall and float, catching a breeze, no doubt startling the driver behind them momentarily, then falling, drifting to the earth as she sped on, her hand still feeling what it felt like to hold that shoe, then suddenly empty, free of the object once more.

And Gay would ride the breeze with that empty hand extended open for a while, reach inside to find another piece of clothing, then extend that windblown arm for another drop, this one 10 miles down the road, creating an odd, unpredictable pattern of small abandoned clothing along their route to confound even the greatest of detectives—even Cannon or Jimmy Rockford or Mannix or Magnum PI—should they be tracking the source of all this abandoned childhood ephemera.

The moment of opening her hand, she said, was pure and total freedom. When she told me the story, I could feel it, too, that hot wind on skin, probably exhilarating because her parents didn't yet know and also because the wind cooled her when it hit the sweat. At the next rest stop, just imagine how surprised her parents were to find her half-naked, shoeless, and smiling in the backseat.

I love that story.

I remember watching an Oprah show where her staff took the studio audience into a room full of left shoes. No right shoes, only the left ones. "They're free," the staffers said, and the studio audience leaped over one another to get those shoes.

No right shoes, only left ones.

It was a show about human behavior when we are offered free things. Many of us become competitive (or worse).

"Why?" Oprah asked when the show started taping and the audience was seated happily in their seats with their left shoes. "Why did you want those left shoes so badly? Do you all have family members at home with one leg?" Many in the audience answered, "We took them because they were there."

What if we don't need all those art supplies, every kind of glue known to man? What could we make happen by creating greater spaciousness so we could really show up like magic?

Always take the train

In complex trains of thought, signs are indispensable. —**George H. Lewes**

There is a languidness to trains that soothes me and makes me slow down, gives me pause, rolls time around in my head and heart and belly at a pace gentler than air travel.

This past week, after two days of work with large, gentle, complex men with Popeye arms who make Sheetrock in Stony Point, New York, I took the train to Washington, DC, rather than flying. What a soothing three hours of rocking

slightly from side to side, sitting into the motion, swaying with it, looking ahead to see a car full of slightly swaying heads and bellies, like seaweed at the ocean's edge or under the pier, swaying, rocking, letting my body feel the motion.

Not correcting it or stopping the motion, that sway, but allowing it, moving with it, a soothing calm, a late-afternoon reverie in deep sun, that special time of day, that warm peace punctuated by strips of sunlight, dappled visions of light, dark, light, dark, light-dark as we moved past trees. It was a peace shattered only by Loud Man on Cell Phone, his voice carrying through the quiet like an arrow piercing the air. "I am a social entrepreneur!" he shouted. "I can't be bothered with this kind of existential trivia!" he continued, using words that made my teeth hurt. "She needs to be fired!" That didn't sound too awfully social, what with his being a social entrepreneur and all.

(As an aside, cell phones are the bane of my existence. I once gathered enough information from another train-bound Mr. Loud to apply for a credit card in his name, should I have wanted to do so: birth date, address, phone numbers, e-mail addresses, Social Security number, mother's maiden name, wife's name and Social Security number, their wedding anniversary date, the site of their past five international trips, their children's names and birthdates, his employer's name and address, and much more. When I realized how extensive a personal history he was broadcasting to his captive audience, I started writing down the information I heard, quietly offering the page to him as I disembarked, with a note suggesting the dangers of Living Out Loud.)

Yes, there is something fulfilling about train travel that airplanes don't offer, a voyeuristic and momentary journey into the lives of people whose homes abut the tracks, realizing with a shock of recognition that whole lives—birth to death—are occurring in those walls we pass. All the things of life: those dinners that sometimes burn, television blue glow hypnosis, disappointments and birthday cakes, birth and rebirth, that precious mundane life, like brushing teeth and inside jokes and watering basil on the windowsill.

Some track dwellers attempt a form of beauty for fellow travelers by decorating their track-focused patios with plants. Some allow for the futility of beautification or privacy: white fences wholly penetrable by my gaze from the track above.

Watchfulness, fast passing, like life is, really, barreling in another direction, away, away. People and circumstances left behind as we step forward to a destination, hoping we're on the right track, the right train, and panicking when we think we are not. How much do we miss by going so fast, I wonder often; how much do we miss by worrying about arriving at the right destination rather than enjoying the view, so quickly passing by; how much do we miss by not stopping to dip into that life, the one in front of us instead of the one ahead of us, by not recognizing that **the destination is really a horizon, not a boundary.**

When I lived in Munich, train travel was like breathing. Going to Italy, Brussels, Amsterdam, Switzerland? By train, of course. Ah, those lovely sleeping cars, those meetings with others, that memorable journey from Munich to Amsterdam perched on small pull-down seats in the corridor for hours with my friend, the fantastic Howard, watching Europe pass by us, making up stories about the people's lives in houses we passed, their fires glowing, their lamps beckoning us on, forgetting momentarily if we were moving or if they were.

Living in Sri Lanka much earlier in life—as a teenager—I took a train from Colombo to a small village down the coast, traveling to attend a Sinhalese wedding, a three-day feast. The tracks took me by the coast, impossibly large coconut and palm trees lining the country's outline, all swept by the wind

It is in rhythm that design and life meet. —Philip Rawson

into amazing arcs over our tracks. The train car in which I found myself was occupied almost entirely by young naval officers, a brilliant brown in their starched white uniforms. Inspired by the palm trees, I started softly singing to myself the theme song to Gilligan's Island, that fateful trip and tiny ship, that three hour tour. Before I reached "the skipper brave and true," the whole train car was singing.

We made our way slowly down that coastline for hours, moving from Gilligan, the professor, and Mary Anne to *My Three Sons* and on to how we all became the Brady Bunch. It was magical, swaying down the coast, singing, laughing, finding a common language; however fictional the reference point. The idea of a single humanity didn't seem too far away that day.

Call me crazy, but I just can't see that happening on a plane (or on the Long Island Rail Road, for that matter).

The train frees us up—or it can. But not if we're there but not there; there but on the phone; there but on our BlackBerry; there but in our laptop; there but resisting the sway and rhythm of the ride.

Enjoying my languid train journey to DC, I was disappointed that I was scheduled to fly home from there, not sway and rock. But fly I did. And on that flight yesterday, I flew with a pilot who enlisted all of us in his fantasy of being a stock-car driver or perhaps a bobsled team captain at 37,000 feet, so sudden were our drops in altitude, so banked were our turns, so fast was our descent, like Mario Andretti had overpowered Vonetta Flowers to take the helm.

A few moments into the flight, we banked a turn so steeply, with me at the bottom of it, that I found myself leaning at a forty-five-degree angle back uphill into the seat of the person beside me, convinced that my rigid counterbalance was the one thing keeping the plane from tipping over, my head in front of the head of Mr. 8B, my every nerve tensed and holding, holding, holding, willing the plane back upright.

How unlike my seaweed-in-water-under-the-pier on that train. How unlike Gilligan and friends, that unspeaking and forward-facing bunch aboard the plane not allowing for song. How small and indistinguishable were the people and their basil plants and patios miles below, not even like ants, so small. Humanity escaped us way up there, my rigidity belied my fear of tipping over, we moved too fast and too small, then.

Take the slow train, not the express. Put down your cell phone. Sing songs with your fellow travelers (even silently) and find the themes, those indispensable signs that we're on the right track, that the track we're on is always the right one. Lean into the turns, not against them. Create a languidness in which relationship and noticing and slow living can flourish.

give yourself 10

Word: In what areas of life are you on the express train? What are the slow trains you need to get on? How can you lean into the slow?

Image: Make an image of your slow train. What do you need to let go of in order to ride that train? The belief that "time is money," for example, keeps us moving quickly even when the counterintuitive action—"slowing down"— is called for.

give yourself 37

Life is a both/and, not either/or proposition. Just as relaxing into the rhythm of your train provides creative space in the form of time and seeing more, so too the disruption of that rhythm can jar us into a more creative space. Change your route every day as you drive home from work or school. Consciously break one of your tracks. Make note of the process each evening. Getting lost slows us down and frees us up. It also disrupts our rhythm, vital to creativity.

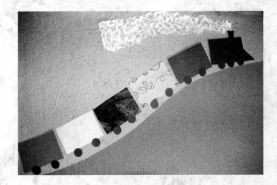

The last time I checked, it was still legal to take long, deep breaths. —Jeff Davidson

Swing slow big arcs

The near stillness recalls what is forgotten, extinct angels. —**Georg Trakl**

One week, the same message came to me from four places: on a table, while driving up Hillside Street, by a bonfire, and watching a tree swing trace its lazy arc.

On a table

She opened the door. "Hi," she said, "it's good to see you." "You, too!" I said. We walked to two identical chairs near the window, black with straight backs, burgundy silk quilted pillows perched on their cushions. We sat down. She opened my file. "What's been happening with you recently?" she asked. "Not much," I answered. "Just traveling every week and doing volunteer work and writing a lot and getting Emma ready for college and planning a 37days retreat and doing some client work and sending out a book proposal and applying for some fellowships and collecting contributions for a charity auction and taking Tess to the park and creating baby kimonos and . . ."

She sat looking at me. "Is that all?" she asked with a smile.

"I guess it does seem like a lot when I list it all," I said. "But I've been cutting back."

"How have you been feeling?" came her reply.

"Pretty well. Just a little tired. And a few headaches. And my lower back hurts a little. But I feel good," I said.

"Have you been taking your Chinese herbs twice a day?" she asked.

Now, as an aside, it occurs to me—perhaps irrationally, but there you have it—that this woman could actually *tell* if I'd been taking my Chinese herbs twice a day. I know it's irrational, but when she took my pulses, it occurred to me that my body betrayed the truth—I had forgotten to drink that warm tea made from herbs. "Not consistently," I admit, figuring that she'll know soon enough anyway. She made a few notes in her file, asked to see my tongue and drew a picture of it, with little spots all over it, like reading tea leaves on some bumpy landing strip. "Let's get you up on the table; I'll be back in a moment."

When she returned, I was resting on the table, looking up at a mobile of swans. **I would pay her every week just to rest on this table, looking at these swans, just for an hour of quiet in a room with no clutter.** Perhaps I should raise the issue with her—would she rent naps? What would be an appropriate pay scale for naps?

When I left DC, there were two people whose loss left me numbed: my dear hairdresser of eighteen years, Rene, a man who kept me a redhead long after reality did, and Susan, my acupuncturist of nearly ten years whose hands always reminded me of a poem by e. e. cummings: "no one, not even the rain, has such small hands." It took me four years to find suitable substitutes, and I knew from the moment I arrived in her office the first time that this acupuncturist—like mine in DC—is a healer.

I closed my eyes, her hands at my wrist, feeling my telling pulses. What was she reading there, I always wondered. Was it possible—as I imagined—for her to tell? That I wasn't drinking enough water, that I didn't get to the gym every day, that my closets were messy, that I wasn't taking my herbs, that I lost my library card, that I ate a Raspberry Frosted Pop-Tart with five grams of fat and 210 calories for breakfast in a moment of weakness, or laziness, or a repudiation of adulthood or common sense? What could she tell during that long silence of reaching for my pulses, my internal dialogue, my blood screaming past that point she held?

"I'd like to do some points on your head and legs today," she said. She worked quietly, the unwrapping of needles a familiar sound; otherwise, quiet. I lost track of where she was, my mind racing, trying to slow itself down, an internal monologue that embarrassed me, it was so pedestrian: *Get apple juice, don't forget cat food, send Emma's health form to school, finalize that handout for Portland, get the contract signed, send a card to Eliav, print photos for Nilanthi and Ajith, pick up the dry cleaning.* I wished the list were more impressive: *Solve world hunger, end racism, build schools for underprivileged youth.* But the fact was that my mind was full of minutiae. (I've been reading about people using a get-things-done method of writing down everything that needs to be done in order to free up their minds, but after buying the book that explained the system, I promptly lost it until John, triumphant at the irony, found it under the bed yesterday. It was nearly as bad as the time that he found *Love It or Lose It: Living Clutter Free Forever* in a dangerously large pile of papers near my desk a few years back.)

Suddenly and without warning, I heard a disembodied voice behind my head: "What are the opportunities for stillness in your life?" she said.

It was a question so shocking and so without an answer that it made me laugh, that reflexive, awful, telling laugh that comes when you are shocked into some kind of cellular recognition, that laugh that isn't really a laugh at all.

While driving

The bicyclist ahead of me seemed wobbly.

With no space to pass him, I stayed respectfully behind, knowing that I wasn't up to the challenge of biking up this hill and so needed to pay my respects to someone who was.

He appeared to be on fire, as well, a slight plume of smoke rising from his right side. *Perhaps it's just steam, after all the humidity is high and he's working hard; I'm sure that's it,* I thought to myself.

I got closer. His body seemed skewed in some way—*what an interesting posture!* I thought. *I wonder if he's more aerodynamic that way? It's amazing what they do with aerodynamics these days! And was that a piece of paper he just dropped? Should I let him know? What if it's something important?*

I was finally able to pass, and as I did, I realized that he was not only biking, but talking on a cell phone and smoking a cigarette at the same time. And, what? He was also eating a Snickers, the wrapping of which he had dropped a few yards before.

How utterly ridiculous! I thought to myself. *How stupid, how dangerous, how unfocused and unproductive and . . . and . . . how like me, eating, e-mailing, watching TV, driving, talking, negotiating, cooking—simultaneously sometimes, never one thing at a time anymore, like the biker.*

Like him, I am on fire, a slight plume of smoke rising from my right side. And not a good fire (see below), but a dangerous one. I'm in danger of dying of smoke inhalation from this fire.

By a fire

Our friends Sweet-Sweet Tina and Big John—as Tess calls them—invited us to a bonfire at their new house in the country last Saturday night. When during our tour of Said House we hit the downstairs "Mediterranean" bathroom, with walls the color of the ocean's depths shimmering with glitter in the glow of small colored bulbs, Emma turned to face me head-on and said in very deliberate tones, "I hate our house."

Aside from Enormous and Unrelenting House Envy, what I discovered in this visit—from sitting by the fire, the sound of crickets buzzing, the threat of bats above, the feel of warm in the front facing the fire and cool in the back, kids running in Rumi's field—was that place where right and wrong meet and have a lovely talk, people sitting around the fire, their presence barely seen across the blaze, soft voices punctuating the quiet then falling silent again, mesmerized by the white flames. Sweet-Sweet Tina had brought a basket of paper and markers for us to write our wishes on, then throw them into the fire and watch them glow. **There wasn't a need for much else in the world, not then. And ever?** Why had it been so long since I had sat like that, roasting in a fire? It was an opportunity for stillness too little taken.

On a swing

We went to a neighborhood potluck picnic at Cate and Ben's house on Sunday, a gathering of people who live in proximity, but many of whom we hadn't met. The highlight for Tess was a simple wooden swing. Hung on a sturdy black rope suspended from a branch more than 20 feet in the air, it produced the most languid, big, slow swing imaginable.

Tess swung an arc of pure joy into a blue sky, thrilled by wind and nurtured by the knowledge that we stood at both ends of the arc to watch over her, see her laugh, and keep her in motion. As I watched, it occurred to me that, like the fire, there are great pleasures in the simplest of things—many of them outside, not by my computer, but in nature, that air, those clouds, that sky, that living, with someone named John at the end of my arc to catch me when I'm falling.

Your creative challenge

Be still. Stop moving. Extract yourself from your evil: that cell phone, your BlackBerry, those piles of undone. Create opportunities for stillness. Or if you can't be still, at the very most swing slowly and in a big arc, high enough to get perspective on what's below. Seeing and knowing are vital to tapping into our creative spirit . . . and they sometimes come from stillness, sometimes from aloneness, sometimes from seeing from a vastly different perspective.

give yourself 10

Word: What are your opportunities for stillness?

Image: Create an image, word, or sign that reminds you to create stillness in your life every day. Paste it on your mirror so you will see it every morning.

give yourself 37

Create ten minutes of stillness every day. There are many ways to create stillness—at synagogue during services amid the singing; sitting in Seat 8C aboard a Boeing 777; taking a walk in a city you don't know; sitting to meditate. Don't limit yourself to quiet solitude— it may never come. Just consistently create the kind of stillness in chaos you can every day. Create a stillness practice. Notice what you notice.

Carve a Chinese chop

We had the experience, but we missed the meaning. —**T. S. Eliot**

Sometimes the lessons we need about living more creatively are simply and beautifully embodied in the people we meet and the relationships we create.

Stay up all night

He looked Chinese. At a break in the workshop, I asked if he was from China. "Yes," he answered. "I'm originally from China."

"Can I ask you a question?" I asked, and so we sat down and I told him a story:

Almost thirty years ago, I was a young administrator in a nonprofit organization in DC that brought a delegation of fifteen college presidents from very remote provinces of China to the United States for a month to visit state colleges.

Because I had taken a year of Chinese language courses at Johns Hopkins University, I was chosen to accompany the group around the United States for that month, traveling to a different state college or university nearly every day. Never mind that I was only fluent in about ten Chinese phrases like "I drink American beer."

Many in the group didn't speak much English, but our young interpreter was a big help, and the mistakes we made were amusing, once we all got comfortable with one another. But there was one young man who spoke no English, a man named Ye Gongxian, president of the Yunnan Arts Institute. Ye Gongxian and I shared some unspoken friendship that grew quickly. When I look at all the photographs of that time together, what I notice most is that he and I are almost always standing or sitting together. So while we shared no common language, we connected at some human level beyond words.

WHAT WE LEARN FROM EXPERIENCE DEPENDS ON THE KIND OF PHILOSOPHY WE BRING TO EXPERIENCE.

—C. S. Lewis

The group learned at dinner one night that I would celebrate my birthday with them. The next morning we waited for Ye Gongxian to arrive at breakfast, but he was uncharacteristically late.

"He'll be here soon," one of the Chinese visitors said. "He was up all night working." In a few moments he arrived, looking as if he had, indeed, not slept, his wiry straight black hair standing in direct opposition to gravity, his simple black jacket wrinkled more than usual.

We went on our way that day, visiting a college. That evening at dinner, he presented me with a small green brocade box. "Happy birthday," he said, trying out his English-language skills long enough to wish me well on my special day. I opened the green box and found an intricately carved dragon on a tall rectangle of marble. I turned it over to find Chinese characters on the bottom.

"He stayed up all night to carve you a Chinese chop," someone said. A "chop" is a stone stamp used in China to serve as your signature, they explained.

"This is a big deal," the young interpreter whispered to me, lest I miss the significance of this famous artist creating a chop for me with the Chinese name he had chosen for me. "A very big deal," he said.

I lost touch with Ye Gongxian. All efforts to reach him led me to a place where I needed more Chinese-language skill than I had to move forward. He was no longer the president of Yunnan Arts Institute. So my question to the man at the workshop was this: "Can you help me find him?"

By the lunch break he had. "Is this the man you mean?" he asked, holding out a photograph he had printed off the Web.

It was.

Like me, he was more than twenty years older, but still him. He's learned a little English now, and we have been in touch ever since. I sign my letters to him with the name he carved so many years before.

> What one has not experienced one will never understand in print.
> —Isadora Duncan

Make it worth it

At sixty-five, Mrs. Smith was as near to ancient as you could be to a fourth grader. But she evidently didn't know that. Kids in my class started yelping one day at the door to our classroom; we all ran to the door to see Mrs. Smith, in her skirt and heels no less, riding someone's spider bike with a banana seat and chopper handlebars down the hallway of the school, her long legs bent nearly in half, a huge grin on her face. She constantly surprised and delighted us in that way—every single day was an adventure—and at the same time it was very clear that she expected every single person to do their best work. And each of us—even the most challenged—rose to the level of her very high expectations.

Once, in a fit of infatuation, I let a little redheaded boy named Bryan copy from my spelling test. Suddenly there was a shadow on my long, thin strip of paper, on which I had written "shoulder, power, turbulence." I looked up to see Mrs. Smith leaning over me, her head cocked to one side. She said only four words. That was all she needed to say. It's all she ever needed to say: "Was it worth it?"

In such a way, she instinctively led us to our own learning rather than mandating it—with the freedom she gave us came great responsibility. **We knew she respected us in that way.** I know that my work as an adult around diversity and "isms" came directly from the ways in which she treated every person with respect, seeking to find the genius in each of us—and finding it. And I know that the joy for life that I write about in my blog and books is a direct descendant of that year in that fourth-grade classroom (and all those years after).

The last time I visited her, she was in her early nineties and my older daughter, Emma, was about six years old. Before I knew it, Mrs. Smith had Emma seated at a table and was showing her how to make a tricorner hat out of newspaper. After they made two hats (one for each of them), she and Emma took off marching down the hallways of her retirement village in their newspaper hats, playing those red-and-beige plastic recorders from my childhood. Her incredible zest for life never left her.

Our classroom bulletin boards were glorious paeans to a big, big world outside. I remember helping her with a bulletin board once about Fontana Dam, on which she made an error, spelling it Fontana Damn. Only after we put up the whole bulletin board did she realize it, laughing and laughing at herself. She expected us to see the world, whether we ever left North Carolina or not. As a class, we read aloud books like *Sixty Seconds Over Tokyo*. She was determined to have us see a world outside the small southern town in which we lived.

Her handwritten note to me at the end of that year said she knew I would grow up to see the world. I did, traveling to more than sixty countries. I sent her a postcard from every single place I traveled. We stayed in touch until she died at ninety-three years old. The last time I visited, she was in a nursing home apartment. In the den, I saw a huge piece of art, a collage. As I got closer, I realized it was every postcard I had ever sent her.

Be a rock fairy

I was invited to more than forty cities when *Life Is a Verb* came out. Not by bookstores, but by readers of my blog. Together we created a fantastic book tour, one beautiful city (and host) at a time.

From the moment the book was published, a woman named Debbie Kelley repeatedly invited me to come to her small town in New Hampshire to read from *Life Is a Verb*. "When I have work in that area," I assured her, "I will definitely come." A speech in Sturbridge, Massachusetts, gave me that chance.

When I got there after a day of Travel Insanity, Debbie had gathered an amazing group of people in a wonderful space. The energy was beautiful, ripe, palpable. I arrived just before the reading was to begin because of the afore-mentioned Travel Insanity, and sat down to catch my breath for a moment. Debbie was adorned with a pink tiara and magic wand with 37DAYS written on them, and she had handed out beautiful birthday cake candles to everyone to celebrate one of the essays in *Life Is a Verb*. It was perfect, I thought as I sat talking to Debbie's husband, Skip.

Perfect.

And then I saw a dark-haired woman walking amid the close-knit tables with a basket that she offered to each person she met. Each peered in, then smiled, and reached in to take something. She stopped by my table with not only the basket, but also a small cellophane bag beautifully tied with multicolored ribbons. "I wanted you to have these," she said.

Inside were beautiful stones she had painted, each a gorgeous hue, each with a simple statement on them: LOVE MORE, BE PRESENT, EAT A CUPCAKE, LEAP!, and more. In addition to the bag of stones, she held out the basket to me. I reached in and took one: "Pain = change," it said. Because of an event the day before in my life, it was perfection to choose that stone.

"You're like a rock fairy!" I said to her.

"Yes," she said, "Yes, I think I am."

Channel Maxine and Elizabeth

I first met Maxine and Elizabeth in a small bookstore in Austin called Bookwoman, where I was doing a reading from *Life Is a Verb*. They drove from Houston to be there. Then they came to North Carolina to a retreat I was hosting with my business partner, David, bringing with them a magical metal box in which were all the necessary ingredients to teach me to knit, along with a notepad they had made me, a book on the Zen of knitting, and a Johnny Depp Pez dispenser. It was love at first sight. Their humor, generosity, and expansive way of seeing the world captured my imagination, as did Elizabeth's story of a community art project they had created for a friend's birthday:

> I asked a group of people if they wanted to be part of a birthday surprise for a friend, Dawn, a wonderful artist and prankster in arms. I drew a picture over a series of watercolor postcards and sent each project participant a postcard. They could then color the card in any manner they saw fit. Then, we would mail the cards starting the Monday before the birthday girl's big day. We had participants in five states, which was good because this meant the cards would arrive at different times during the week. Everyone sent their card in an envelope as opposed to sending it as

a postcard mainly because of the wear and tear it might go through at the post office.

During that week, Dawn told me the first one came and she thought how sweet of so and so to send her a birthday card. Then the second one arrived and she figured something was up. After that, she delighted in getting the mail to see what card arrived next. It was great fun for all involved.

But that wasn't the end. Dawn and her wife Lisa decided to send the finished project around to everyone who participated. They got a bunch of T-shirts made, put the finished postcards in a velvet pouch, put it all in a box, and sent the box out with instructions that whoever received the box would then send it along to another participant.

We were the first stop on the "box tour." Maxine put a journal into the box for people to write in any thoughts they had. I painted a face on the box. I then took the box on a trip to Virginia to visit two of the other artists. From there the box was sent around the country to the rest of the artists. Every now and then Dawn and Lisa would ask about the box. No one knew who had the box at any given time. There was no discussion of its whereabouts. Everybody kept it a secret.

In February of 2008, we decided to go to Connecticut to visit Dawn and Lisa for a party with a group of friends—six of the other postcard artists would also be at the party. Two of the postcard artists also live in Connecticut, one of whom, Ann, was hosting the party. Ann e-mailed me two days earlier and said she had the box. She was the final house on the "box tour." The convergence of us in Connecticut at the same time the box arrived at her house could only be described as "the universe in motion." It was the perfect storm of communal collaboration.

At this time, everyone knew about the box except Dawn and Lisa. About halfway through the party, we brought out the box. Dawn screamed with

I'm not a genius. I'm just a tremendous bundle of experience. —Buckminster Fuller

delight. People had added things to the box, written in the journal and on the box. In the end it was an art journey of grand proportions and a wonderful testament to what a group of people can create with some markers, crayons, and a little imagination.

In Maxine and Elizabeth's world, **every day is a communal art project, each hour an opportunity for artistic generosity.**

Your creative challenge

Be an angel for someone. Who needs you to stay up all night and carve a chop for them? Give them your gift—your time, a special name to let you know you see them, a chop. Look for opportunities to bring people together around a shared project or vision—and let them take it where they will.

give yourself 10

Word: What does "community" look like to you? What is your ideal community?

Image: Identify the gift you most need to offer—and to whom. Make an image of that gift.

give yourself 37

Sometimes our gifts take the form of knitting boxes and sometimes they are "invisible." My friend Lora Abernathy makes three simple peace offerings each day (sharing her umbrella, letting someone into traffic ahead of her, opening the door for someone, and the like). They may never know it, but she does. Do the same for 37 days and notice the reaction—in you, and in the recipient. If you are so inclined, follow the lead further and create artfulness that you offer to the world in some way each day for 37 days—a chop, a postcard, a story.

Sit still with Slumpy

He moves nice. It's his stillness that's not right. —**Marilyn Whirlwind**

Years ago, I was on I-40, driving from Greensboro, North Carolina, to a small town several hours west of there, when I heard a loud bang, an explosion, then a deafening sharp scary ongoing *thump, thump, bang, thump.* I started to lose control of the car. And as I watched in horror, the black rubber from the rear tire of my happy Oldsmobile 88 started spinning up into the atmosphere, pieces hitting like gunshots against the rim and wheel of the car, then spinning, twirling, perfect little eddies of centrifugal force, away from the car, off the tire they were supposed to support, large hunks of rubber getting smaller, smaller, gone. I veered wildly to the side of the road; the tire was essentially gone. I could imagine it wheeling its way into space, tiny bits of rubber spiraling upward.

It feels as if the same thing has been happening over the past few weeks; the pieces that are flinging into the universe are not tire rubber but something else, like life caught in the whirling of an old-fashioned metal fan, the kind without a child guard, with slats wide enough for whole bodies to go through into that whirling dervish of metal and wind, the kind we used before we decided to make everyone else responsible for our own safety. First my beautiful eighteen-month Moleskine date book on which my entire life is written and cataloged, all those due dates and appointments and trips and to-dos and fabulous ideas for future essays, gone. Twirled off into the universe like a comet burning itself out. This last loss of my calendar was one of three such losses and re-finds over the past few months. "I wonder what that means," my wise acupuncturist Hannah said last week. "That you keep losing your calendar. Any idea what that means?" she asked in that voice that indicates for all the world to hear that she knows what it means. This, you might remember, is the same woman who shocked me with the question, "What are the opportunities for stillness in your life?"

Then my camera. My beautiful, fast, wonderful, new, beloved Canon Digital Elph PowerShot SD600 digital camera. Gone. On the desk, then gone. Did I lose it on a trip? Did Tess throw it away? Did it fling itself into the universe to find my Moleskine? I can't afford to replace it now, so I suppose I am left to actually look at the world myself, remember it myself, not rely on a camera's eye. That's a lesson I'd prefer to read about, thank you, than experience.

And so, over the past few weeks, this centrifugal force has been flinging things away from me at an alarming pace, things I thought vital to my existence. But as Elisabeth Kübler-Ross said of her house burning down, **I could either see the loss as completely paralyzing or as completely liberating, and I've chosen the latter.**

If I have an appointment with you, I don't know it. If I'm supposed to be somewhere at a certain time, I have no clue about that. I am free, blissfully ignorant of the frenetic pace to which I had committed my Self, my days unencumbered by little one-hour time blocks. I hate being late, which makes this latest loss significant, and when added to my recent denial of watches (with apologies to the nice man named David whom I met on a flight recently and who owns a watch company), time consciousness has been brought to a whole new level.

I am, essentially, out of the Everydayathon.

But evidently, even after the date book and camera, I still had some learning to do.

On a Thursday night in Albuquerque, I fell. And I fell hard. I'll let you choose the story you like best: (1) I was saving a child from a burning building; (2) I was dancing the tango with an aging interculturalist at a conference of aging interculturalists like me; or (3) I fell off a curb I did not see. There was no stumble, no hesitation, no trying to stop the fall—I did not anticipate the impact because I didn't see it coming. I just went down, hard and fast, to the ground, landing on my left knee and the heels of my palms. My business partner, David, and I were in Albuquerque to conduct a workshop the next morning at a conference; he rushed to my side when he heard the impact. The pain immediately made me nauseous as I struggled to get in the car. He drove. Being the polite accident victim I am, I focused on not vomiting from the pain.

We finally found a hospital. Eight hours and a lot of swelling later, we emerged at 3:30 a.m. with a lot of emergency room stories and characters, a prescription for painkillers (not the painkillers themselves, mind you), a splint, and the best wishes of Dr. Victory, a sleep-deprived intern with a penchant for repetitive, seemingly irrelevant questions and long, unexplained absences. After a futile search for an all-night pharmacy, we arrived back at the hotel at 4:00 a.m. Ibuprofen would have to do until morning came. It's the first time I've ever arrived in my hotel room *after* they put the bill under the door. Our wake-up calls were at 6:30 a.m. to present our session.

That was a short night. It was, more exactly, a non-night.

Turns out, Yeats was right—things do fall apart, the center cannot hold.

The outcome? I had many opportunities for stillness in my life for a good long while. In fact, my life was One Big Opportunity For Stillness. With no calendar and no way to walk, Stillness Loomed. Nothing But Stillness. All Stillness, All the Time.

After our session, we drove north of Albuquerque to work, my club of a foot on the dashboard in its brace and conspicuous orthopedic white sock, held

up by hope that the swelling wouldn't cause the skin to burst, and buoyed—finally—by Vicodin.

An hour into our trip, suddenly, a loud gunshot rang out, glass shards peppered our clothing, a projectile forced its way toward us, through the glass. We swerved, then righted ourselves, shaken, looking at each other and trying to figure out what had just happened. A large rock had hit the windshield of the rental car, sending glass into our laps. *Okay, enough messages from the universe. I give up. Stillness, it is.*

In the absence of my very favorite nurse, my very own husband, my business partner David did an admirable job of applying ice packs, bringing food objects, and wagging a crooked finger at me to keep my leg elevated. The leg kept me still; the lack of Internet access and the canyon-induced cell phone outage provided the total disconnect. Just the trees.

After a day of reclining on a couch in gorgeous Jemez Springs, New Mexico, with golden cottonwood trees blowing in the breeze outside, napping in and out of a Vicodin haze, and watching my ankle swell to the size of my head, I traveled home at the mercy of those nice people in airports who push people in wheelchairs from one gate to another, or not. You'll be happy to know that not one inch of my body—and especially the suspicious, swollen ankle bits—went unswabbed by that gunpowder explosives checker swab thing at security. Meanwhile, buckets full of Purell and shaving cream and exploding toothpaste were whizzing by behind the security guards—like that Lucille Ball episode when she's working in a chocolate factory—without being inside a requisite quart-size clear zip-lock bag.

When I got home, Emma carried my bags for me, John swept me into the house, and Tess covered me up with her blankie and started bringing me piles of her books to read: *The Okay Book* and *"I Can't," Said the Ant*.

Then she disappeared upstairs, coming down minutes later with a proud smile and, in her outstretched hand, Slumpy, a much-treasured bright-pink-and-yellow monkey who started his life in our house seventeen years ago when Emma was small. And so, I sat quietly with my vast opportunities for stillness, me and Slumpy, my Vicodin, and a book about a wizard named Harry. Join us.

Your creative challenge

As D. H. Lawrence wrote, **"One's action ought to come out of an achieved stillness: not to be mere rushing on."** Stop running the Everydayathon. Sit very, very still with Slumpy. The universe is telling you to slow down—how? What is blowing away from you with some strong centrifugal force? Are you listening, or are you disregarding the messages? Because if you are dissing the universe, it will get you. Not today, maybe, and not tomorrow, but someday soon you're not going to see that curb. And then, my friend, you're going to be sitting still for a long, long time.

Don't merely rush on. Your center cannot hold.

give yourself 10

Word: How is the universe telling you to slow down? What's thwarting your desire to rush?

Image: What is your Slumpy, that thing you hold on to in moments of stillness? Draw it. Let that be your reminder to slow, slow.

give yourself 37

Listen to the universe for 37 days and make notes. Answer the phone of the universe. If you are stuck in traffic, that's the universe telling you to be still. Interpret it as such (rather than getting angry, as you are actually receiving a gift). List the ways in which you are being told to slow down, whether you take that advice or not.

ONE'S ACTION OUGHT TO COME OUT OF AN ACHIEVED STILLNESS: NOT TO BE A MERE RUSHING ON.

—D. H. Lawrence

Find Miss Florence Painter

We read to know we are not alone. —**C. S. Lewis**

The Bermuda Triangle that has sucked up into its awful vortex my favorite fountain pen, my copy of *Getting Things Done* (ironic, isn't it?), and my beautiful Canon Elph PowerShot SD600 digital camera has continued to grow in scope and intensity and greediness and sheer audacity. My winter coat, the right shoe to my favorite Merrell clogs from the Old North State Clothing Company, and the TV remote control are now gone. I haven't seen my special highlighter in a week, the recipe for Gay's mother's pimiento cheese is AWOL, and there have been no sightings of my button collection in quite some time. I lost my right crutch yesterday, but found it this morning in a place even I couldn't have imagined, which made me feel really terrible and small for secretly believing that the UPS man had stolen it from the front porch. I've hidden my favorite Moleskine and Zebra 0.7mm Cadoozles Fun Pencil to save them from the Centrifugal Fury.

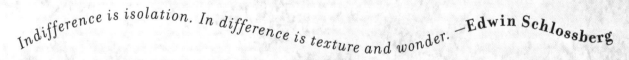

My friend Rosemary insists that the camera and remote are in our family room; if they are, they are hiding quite assiduously. Losing the camera was devastating. I might have mentioned that once or twice or twelve times. But losing that remote control is the best thing that has ever happened to us. Except for missing *Whose Line Is It Anyway?* and all those lovely animated Burl Ives–induced Frosty the Snowman movies, that tremendously cute if ornery Dr. House, the wonderful animated kids' show *Charlie and Lola,* and Kyra Sedgwick's glorious southern accent in *The Closer,* we are happier without it. Oh sure, at first we sat pecking at the cable box like barnyard chickens on crack, desperately trying to change channels without a knob, but then **we realized we could just turn the TV off and move on to other things**, like re-creating the penultimate scene in Uccello's *Battle of San Romano* in macaroni, or something more low-carb, like reading books.

When I was a child, I begged to be allowed to read in bed and was told that I could, until time for lights out. Then, to thwart my parents' wishes that I be

Indifference is isolation. In difference is texture and wonder. —**Edwin Schlossberg**

well rested rather than well read, I would sneak and read under my covers, sitting up so my head formed the apex of a blankie tent, illuminated from within as if a brilliant blaze was consuming the covers, using a flashlight to continue romping through Mrs. Piggle Wiggle's latest adventure—perhaps the one on the farm!—until all hours of the night. I was sure it would fool them when they peered in and could see only the miraculous glowing bed tent, but inevitably the Long Arm of the Law caught up with me.

"You'll ruin your eyes," my mother would wail. "You'll ruin your eyes." Given that I was already practically legally blind and wearing really ugly bifocals by the time I was nine, I reasoned with her: "I wouldn't have to risk their further ruin if you would listen to logic and let me read until I weep with exhaustion." My initial attempts at lawyerly reasoning were futile. No go. Lights out.

I had learned to read at four, well before starting school because my brother was in first grade and already reading; I refused to be left behind. I was also desperate to learn how to write my name—the only thing standing between me and my own library card was being able to write my whole name myself. Having scaled that hurdle, finally, there were years of Pippi and Encyclopedia Brown and all those little biographies of famous people to look forward to!

Mama took me to the library every week without fail, holding like the Holy Grail my little orange library card with the metal ID number on it, tucking and retucking it intently inside its beautiful little green paper slipcase. I still have that card. I even have my original application for it, written in a gorgeous five-year-old handwriting, crooked and exaggerated, those two *t*'s towering above the *a* like redwood overlords, a large doughnut for a dot over the *i*. I'm sure the card and application are here somewhere. Perhaps they're with my clog.

> I have no special talents. I am only passionately curious.
> —Albert Einstein

When I got old enough to work, I finally got a job there. Just imagine the absolute thrill of riding that Bookmobile, taking books to the unwashed masses!

The tallest three humans in this house are Big Readers, Emma most of all. She reads so much—in daylight, under a blankie tent with a flashlight—that she puts me and John to shame. Tess is making impressive efforts. Even at three years old, she could do a pretty convincing rendition of her book about Gus the Troll who has a beautiful voice and isn't especially good looking, but I think she was faking it. Emma learned to read in the first grade under the graceful tutelage of Miss Jones, a wonderful young woman from South Africa who was her first teacher at the Washington International School.

The reading primers they used were British, the Oxford Reading Tree series illustrated by a man named Alex Brychta, complete with main characters named Biff and Kipper. Emma was so enamored of reading and of the small spectacles that appeared in each of Brychta's illustrations, tucked into a corner, but there in each picture. "Why does he have those eyeglasses in every picture?" she asked.

"I don't know, buddy," John replied. "Why don't we call the man who painted the pictures and find out?"

And so they did. Big John and little six-year-old Emma looked up Alex Brychta, found his phone number in London, and gave him a little ringy-dingy.

He was shocked. When he regained his composure, he very nicely told Emma all about the eyeglasses. It was to be the first of many such interactions for Emma. In fact, she assumed as a result that one was intended to correspond with all authors and artists, and her next conquest was an extended and delightful correspondence with a writer named Twig George. In the second grade, Emma was assigned to do a report on George's *A Dolphin Named Bob,* so she, of course, expected that she would interview the author. Don't we all?

In that way, she is truly John's daughter, a man who called the White House pastry chef to find out how to make a gingerbread castle, who called Clyde Barrow's sister, Kurt Gödel's psychiatrist, the janitor who cleaned up the Rosenbergs' execution chamber, and countless others. He called Hans Bethe once, who—at age ninety-five—answered his own phone.

"Everybody talks," he told me, **"if you come up with an interesting enough question."** I was going to have lunch with the beautiful and talented writer Carlos Fuentes once and John learned through transcripts of past interviews that Fuentes had a beloved second-grade teacher who was formative in his life. Her name was Miss Florence Painter. Many of us mere mortals might have stopped there, but not John. No, he tracked down that teacher. She had died, but we talked to her relatives, a series of calls and conversations about Carlos as a child that led me to an extraordinary welcome from Fuentes and his own fascinating stories of his childhood. He was thrilled to hear his teacher's name, all these years later.

We are a family of seekers, it turns out, empowered by John to call anyone and everyone.

When I first traveled to Stockholm on a business trip, I had one thing in mind: ditch the fascinating and no doubt life-altering conference on modern human resources measurement systems and find the Holy Grail. Go to the place where Astrid Lundgren lives and stand in front of her house. Lundgren was, of course, the creator of my childhood she-ro, Pippi Longstocking. By the time I was in Stockholm, she was very old and not to be bothered. And so I just stood there, looking at her house.

Throw your TV remote away and be a book fool. Read, write in the margins, talk to people about the books you read. Create interesting questions. Find Miss Florence Painter, your favorite writer's second-grade teacher. Talk to her, or people who knew her. Follow the thread.

give yourself 10

Word: According to Marvin Bell, there is a poem behind the poem, questions under the questions. What thread of inquiry are you interested in following? List the five topics that interest you the most, the ones that make your ears perk up when you hear them, the things that break your heart wide open, perhaps.

Image: What does curiosity look like to you? What thread do you most want to follow? Create an image of it, something that will spur you to question, seek, follow the impulse and the thread.

give yourself 37

Each day for 37 days, go deeper into someone else's story. Get *their* story, not yours. This requires listening and asking questions, but not to redirect their story to your own. Be conscious of following the thread, of pushing past that point of curiosity that feels normal to you. How curious is a child? How can you embody that respectful curiosity as an adult? Pay attention to how you feel asking questions.

Blow bubbles every day

There are times when fear is good. It must keep its watchful place at the heart's controls. There is advantage in the wisdom won from pain. —**Aeschylus**

We are deep into bubbles at my house.

Blowing them, taking baths in them, catching them, looking at the colors in them, you name it—bubbles are big news here. Colorful "Fun Bubbles" bottles decorate our porch and punctuate our landscape so that at any turn, your desire to launch a few can be realized.

Late one afternoon Tess and I went out in the backyard to indulge in this obsession. We were just outside the door, on our small deck. After eighty-seven-degree temperatures the day before, this was a day rising only into the fifties and feeling colder with the wind. None of which stopped Tess—she was bubble-focused.

She likes to blow bubbles and then run after them, holding her little plastic bubble wand out in front of her like a landing gear, hoping to touch one of them so it will swirl and come to a resting place atop the circle of plastic from which it was born, a precarious balance of birthing and holding on—I know the feeling.

It was freezing in the brisk wind and I told her I'd be right back, that we needed our coats hanging just inside in the dining room.

The dining room is one room away from where we were; I ran in to get the coats and ran back.

And when I came back, there was an empty space where Tess had been, a void, a lack, a hole, a visible tear in the universe, a jagged edge, a tangible and irreducible loss. "Tess!" I yelled, looking quickly to the most likely place she would have gone—the swing set. Nothing. As I ran farther into the yard, I saw it—that moment of panic and dread emerging—the back gate was open; she was gone.

It happened in ten seconds; that was all it took. My Tess was gone.

How often had I heard that awful phrase on *America's Most Wanted* when parents tell of their child being abducted from a park as they sat ten feet away?—"I turned my head and he was gone." How often had I ridiculed them in my mind, knowing it must have been longer periods of disregard that caused the tragedy. And now, I knew. It was ten seconds—that was enough. She was gone. My beautiful, funny, smart, strong-willed Tess was gone. She was gone in an instant, a quiet and reverberating instant that I would relive forever, changing it in my mind with each reliving to alter this awful outcome.

I dropped the coats and ran to the gate that opens onto the driveway and into the street, screaming her name like a madwoman, limbs akimbo, face hot with fear. She wasn't there. She wasn't there.

She wasn't there.

She wasn't there.

I ran past the car on the driveway to the street, knowing in my heart of hearts that she was gone, that someone had snatched her from the yard in those ten seconds; my heart was bursting, I felt nauseous, I was sick and shaky and full of dread and instantaneous horrible regret that swept through me filling me with bile. As I flew down the driveway, I saw two men walking past; I turned, following their gaze to a point behind me—there was Tess standing resolutely at the back of the car, waving to the passersby and yelling "Hi, fancy people!" as she made her way to the street.

I wonder where she was going, what she was thinking. How unlike her big sister she is. Emma as a small child was reserved and rule-conscious and reticent; raising Tess is like being mother to a 38-inch-tall Janis Joplin. There is a bright shining glory in her immediate reaction to the world; there is also danger and fear, the possibility of glory turning to molten flame and ash.

My relief was intense, the kind where knees buckle, but after my initial long thankful hug as I swooped her into my arms, that relief emerged as anger: "Don't you ever do that again!" the anger at myself displaced onto her. She slumped, her excellent adventure chastised. Like our dog, Blue, who escaped one memorable afternoon for a glorious free romp in the creek, Tess was out there in the world, making her way, marching with her back straight and tiny legs propelling her into the universe, her arms pumping like a cartoon of a walk, a

TRUST IS TRANSCENDENT, RESOLUTE, UNIVERSAL, SACRED AND TOLERANT.

—Gurumayi Chidvilasananda

strong and resolute self. And now, for some unknown reason, I was yelling at her for it. Life is confusing.

It takes only a moment of disregard, of inattention, to lose everything we have, all that we love. And I mean that in the most metaphoric way possible—only a moment, just ten seconds, gone.

I'm one of the most cautious mothers I know, to the sheer and total disappointment of my teenager. When we moved from Washington, DC, I brought with me my understanding of city life and the need for constant vigilance. Emma had never crossed a street alone until we moved here. I have thwarted her schemes to hang out at the mall unchaperoned, long wondering what life will be like when I don't know where she is every moment of the day. I pay attention, I question, I hold on, I touch lightly but firmly.

And yet, sometimes, there are things precious to us that we let go of and they are gone. Perhaps it is a child, or our health, or fitness, or creativity, or passion, or a partner or spouse—we stop paying attention for what seems like ten seconds, but is more like years—and they are gone, snatched from the yard or leaving of their own accord, they are gone.

A strong believer in the power of independence, keeping watch for me doesn't mean keeping tabs or smothering, but being watchful in the fullest sense, paying attention, holding and cherishing, attending to, recognizing that disregard can lead to tragedy. Whether a child or a love or a creative Self, it's important work, that.

And yet, having two girls at such different ages reminds me that **watchfulness changes as we move through time**, that what is watchful for a six-year-old is smothering to a seventeen-year-old, that the kind of freedom teenagers need to make their own decisions and mistakes can be deadly for a first-grader, that our watchfulness over ourselves and others must change and grow.

It turns out that bubbles are the perfect metaphor for this, aren't they? They make their own way in the world, blowing in the wind. We must let them go if they are to move into the sky; they are fragile yet resilient, beautiful only in flight. There is a paradox with bubbles—and with people—as my mother cross-stitched for Emma when she was born: We must give them roots and we must also give them wings.

Bubbles don't exist in the bottle, do they? What are your artistic bubbles? And mine? What would you run with panic at losing? Pay attention to that thing with all your heart. Blow bubbles. Watch them fly. Know how to create them, appreciate their beauty, let them go. And pay attention. Those ten seconds are suddenly a year, then two, then ten, then a lifetime.

give yourself 10

Word: What are your bubbles? The ones you most love? What are the ones you need to release? What fears arise for you when you think about releasing them?

Image: Draw what you most fear losing.

give yourself 37

Be conscious of blowing those bubbles in some way every day for 37 days—what does that look like, feel like, represent for you—in concrete terms? Blow bubbles every day for 37 days and capture their beauty in some way. The creative spark often comes from letting go.

I AM INTERESTED IN MAKING THE SIMPLE PROFOUND, SO MY OWN BACKYARD CAN BE INSPIRATIONAL. I JUST WALK OUT MY DOOR AND IT'S ALL THERE. BY PAINTING SIMPLY, MAGIC HAPPENS.

—Peter Fiore

CHAPTER SEVEN

Catch Fire: *Please Lick the Art*

Technique alone is never enough. You have to have passion. Technique alone is just an embroidered pot holder. —**Raymond Chandler**

Emma and Tess are my greatest teachers about creativity, bar none. Any child can be. Just watch them use their whole arm when coloring, their mouth twisted into concentrated glee. *Abandon* is the word that comes to mind.

Once when David and I were preparing for a retreat, we sat at the picnic table in my backyard, carefully gessoing the covers of journals for each participant to use as their "canvas" during the retreat. Brushstrokes carefully up and down. Brushstrokes carefully side to side. As the journal covers dried in the sun, Tess bounded from the house to join us. "WHAT ARE YOU DOING?" she screamed. "I WANT TO DO THAT!" she screamed, without waiting for the answer to her first question.

"Come on," David said. "Here's a notebook you can paint on."

Be fully passionate about something.
Let your heart be moved.
Know what you love.
Shout it for others to hear.
write—sing, paint, live—
like your hair's on fire.

She sat down beside him and immediately picked up a brush, dipped it in color, and started painting. No design with a careful pencil first, no thinking

It's a lot harder to paint nothing than to paint something. —Graham Gillmore

about color combinations, no fear of perfection, but just strong, passionate impulse to express herself in color.

"Just look at that boldness," David said.

The lines in a coloring book stop us. They rein us in. But they don't stop children. To a child, the lines are just there, not as barrier but—simply—as line.

How do the lines keep color out?

What are the lines in your life that keep color out?

When *Life Is a Verb* was published, one reviewer mentioned that I write like my hair's on fire. I can't imagine a review that would make me happier. That sense of urgency and aliveness and fire and passion—yes! The challenge is keeping that space of clarity and passion and fire open, freed up from the fires of criticism and comparison.

Be passionate in your life. The passion in your art will follow.

THEY TEACH YOU THERE'S A BOUNDARY LINE TO MUSIC. BUT MAN, THERE'S NO BOUNDARY LINE TO ART.

—Charlie Parker

FedEx leaves to someone

We are minor in everything but our passions. —**Elizabeth Bowen**

Only when we get to a certain age can we begin to see patterns in our lives, those choices made and not made, just as we have to be a certain distance from the earth to see crop circles, or SOS spelled out on the beach in coconut husks by Gilligan, or particle tracks.

Some patterns are big and noticeable, like the way Chuck Knoblauch used to screw up his face and fasten and refasten those batting gloves waiting for the pitch, always the same, a pattern anyone could see. And some patterns are small, unnoticeable to the naked eye, like the way I oh-so-subtly reach for Rice Krispie Treats when I'm stressed.

And so it is, from this vantage point of years and distance, that I have discovered one of those subtle patterns that make up our days. As shocking as it will be to you, dear reader, I have discovered that I have a penchant for men named Johnny.

Johnny Appleseed, Johnny Unitas, Johnny Cash, Johnny Depp, and—most important—my own Mr. Brilliant, a man named, yes, Johnny.

It is this last Johnny for whom we baked a heart-shaped red velvet cake smothered in sprinkles for Father's Day, and **it is this last Johnny that I most adore, who is my heart, my love, the man who makes me laugh, who sends me leaves and flowers wherever I am around the world,** who takes Emma out with the telescope to see the stars, who makes architectural structures out of doughnuts and candles for Tessie's breakfast, who wears diapers on his head while singing Tom Waits songs, who decorates the house like Streamer and Balloon Man on crack for birthdays, who tapes lit candles to his head to make us all laugh.

We had an auspicious beginning, me and Johnny.

Years ago, when I checked into my hotel in Copenhagen, it was early morning. I was unprepared for the greeting I received there; suddenly, as I said my name, a phalanx of desk clerks appeared, all smiling and nodding in my direction. "So this is Ms. Digh!" one of them exclaimed to the others. "We've all been waiting for you!"

I was mystified. Up all night on the flight over, I wondered quickly if I was hallucinating. Sure, I was in Copenhagen for a fascinating conference on modern human resources practices—my God, the sheer beauty of that thought—but even so, I couldn't imagine that this fact warranted such a reception. I should have known.

Everywhere I traveled in the world, flowers greeted me. Not tidy predictable baskets of 1-800-Flowers, but big odd beautiful gushing bouquets of unusual wild amazing flowers awaiting me in my room with a note that would both thrill me and make me laugh a big, jet-lagged laugh.

John the Science Boy, as he was called because of his scientific bookshop, charmed front desk staffs in Moscow and Helsinki and Zagreb and Zurich and far beyond, not only getting them to order fantastical bouquets, but sometimes even convincing front desk clerks with no hotel gift shop to go out on their lunch hour to find a favorite magazine like *The Economist* (or, okay, let's be honest: *People* magazine), buy it, bring it back to the hotel, and not only hold it for me, but pre-assign my room, put it under the pillow of the bed with a truffle or Kit Kat bar, and arrange the flowers in the room for me.

After Emma was born, he would even get them to create a smaller bouquet with a note from her, too, and later still, Tess. Sometimes there were six bouquets of varying sizes: one from him, one from Emma, one from each cat and dog, all with cards in handwriting that suited the giver: paw prints, for example, or typography that looked like scratch marks. **How he got strangers all over the world to do these things, I'll never know.**

On one memorable trip, I arrived into Stockholm at o'dark thirty in the morning and the young sleepless woman at the front desk smiled broadly, producing from beneath the counter an exquisitely detailed painting of flowers on an old piece of wood. "There was no florist open nearby," she explained in her beautifully accented English. "So I painted this for you. It is from Johnny the Scientific Boy."

It had started simply with leaves. Autumn leaves.

My friend Gay remembers it this way:

WE SHOULD NOT FORGET TO ENJOY THE EXPERIENCE OF DAILY CREATIVITY, WHATEVER THAT MAY ENTAIL.

—Diane Carter

Fall in Washington is always wonderful; it's such a leafy city and some years the tree-lined streets are literally blazing with color. The first fall that John the Science Boy and Patti got together was one of our more brilliant seasons of color. And she missed it. As I recall, she was in London on business. And the man sent her autumn leaves by Federal Express because he didn't want her to miss that gorgeous Washington fall. He was living on Mintwood Place and that fall, Mintwood Place was particularly gorgeous. Walking from the bus stop on Columbia Road, you passed under a canopy of reds, yellows, and oranges and it would have been hard to be so in love and not want to share those leaves with that person who made your heart hurt when she was away from you. But wanting to share and actually figuring out how to make that happen is what separates the men from the boys. And in this case . . . the man sent her leaves! Did I mention that I was married at the time—still am—to a great guy, and I remember saying that John the Science Boy was a man to leave your husband for. I was basing that mostly on the way that he smelled . . . a mingling of Fahrenheit cologne and old books. But when Patti met Rosemary and me at the Tabard Inn once she had returned from London . . . and, without a word emptied the FedEx packet out onto the little table . . . spreading the leaves before us with one sweeping motion . . . well, that sealed it. We pumped her for more information about the Science Boy. After all, we barely knew him and we wanted details, but she didn't tell us a damn thing. It didn't matter. The man sent her leaves.

Rosemary remembers it this way:

My exact quote was "The man sent her leaves!" as you silently opened up your shoulder bag, removed a FedEx envelope and calmly spread the colorful fall leaves out on the tabletop, fanning them with your long fingers and beautiful nails . . . all of this without a word in response to our heated entreaties: "Patti, how is he, what's the scoop, tell us, tell us all now!" We could barely breathe from the romance.

He still sends me leaves. He is the craziest, funniest, most dear man on the planet. So there, Johnny Depp. Step back.

Those leaves from many years ago are in a shadow box on our wall now, saved for the memory of that extraordinary action, the one that made me gasp in London, and that made Rosemary and Gay gasp when I got home. FedEx leaves to someone. **Create surprise.** Or since the season—at least in this hemisphere—might not support the gathering of leaves at the moment, send something of yourself instead. A seasonal, fleeting piece of your life that you want to share.

> The creation of art is the passion.
> **—Jeffrey Breslow**

give yourself 10

Word: May you have many bouquets in your life. And may you give many bouquets to others. Identify three people who need to hear from you.

Image: What's right in front of you that you could send to those three people? Create an image and send . . .

give yourself 37

Write a thank-you note every day to someone. I started this practice in August 2009, and it is transformative. Find something every day that you feel deserves a thank-you note. I just wrote one to Delta Air Lines for taking me above the clouds for millions of miles and not once crashing a plane I was in. I wrote one yesterday to a young eight-year-old boy I read about in the news who noticed a lost five-year-old and stayed with her until she was reunited with her family. There are things to be thankful for every single day. Seeking them out is a creative act. Responding is life-enhancing for both parties.

Be like Mary Alice

Artists are among the most generous of people. Perhaps inherent in the appreciation of creativity comes a deep, underlying love of humanity and our Earth. —**Kelly Borheim**

It was late when we got to Mary Alice's house. I don't think she knew we were coming. And it didn't seem to matter. At all.

It has been years now, so I can't remember each detail. But the sense I had of that space is still so strong—from out of a dark night we entered into color. Pure color. The house wasn't brightly lit, and yet color stood out. It was the first time I had ever been in a house that was fully, completely, totally someone's. **It was somehow hard to tell where Mary Alice began and ended, the house was so much a part of her.** I remember vivid color and art in unexpected places—not just on the walls, but also on the furniture, floors, ceilings. It seemed absolutely magical to me, with nooks and crannies and lovely bits.

It freed me up somehow, to imagine taking four walls and making them into a full expression of myself.

Mary Alice was a painter, an artist, someone—it seemed to me—who lived life completely on her own terms. Years ago, when Emma was little, a group of friends would meet up for wonderful afternoon garden parties in the village of Waterford, and Mary Alice would be there, her artist's eye working, later creating paintings that captured the sense of the day, as we made hand-cranked lavender ice cream and ate risotto and chocolate tortoni out of martini glasses. Mary Alice had an uncanny way of capturing something clarifying about the people she painted. My friends Gay and Rosemary gifted me years ago with a painting Mary Alice had made of Emma after one of those

Joy is not dependent on circumstances. —**Faith Duck**

afternoons, so perfectly capturing Emma's way of being in the world, her look, that look I still recognize in her, her quiet way of playing.

Mary Alice died years after that first visit to her house, less than a week after a brain aneurysm felled her. As Mary Oliver wrote in a poem, "When Death Comes," Mary Alice was a bride to amazement, to the end.

Her cousin and my friend Gay Clyburn remembered her in achingly beautiful detail:

She studied for a Russian exam in our guest bedroom in Greensboro. Russian. I couldn't imagine anyone so brilliant. She sent me the Kingston Trio Hungry *album and I memorized every song. I was her maid of honor in her wedding to George. I had no idea what I was supposed to do, but it didn't matter. She let me wear anything I wanted. So, it was dotted Swiss with daisies, not her style at all. I remember that she looked beautiful.*

She made my high school graduation gift; it was a brightly colored (orange, red, yellow) découpage trash can filled with things that I might need in college. I kept it through two marriages until it got wet and fell apart. It was the first of many, many Mary Alice gifts that were beautiful works of art, some useful, others just beautiful: rocks, benches, cards, little boxes.

When I first heard the horrible news, I took stock of what was around me in the house at that very moment, things that would keep her with me: six paintings, six watercolor-and-ink cards, a framed photograph, two painted rocks, a bench, a flying painted bird, a little box with crystals in it, a metal snake, a wood carving of a naked man, a used Italian leather notebook, a book of Mary Oliver poems, eight tiny pottery bowls, a bright purple robe, a painted slate "mural." She painted our bathroom on Calvert Street in DC with flowers and vines. In order to finish it while we were away on a trip, she had to paint all through the night while our dog Max slept because during the day she was engaged in throwing a tennis ball a thousand times on demand.

I HOPE I HAVE GIVEN BACK HALF THE JOY MUSIC HAS GIVEN ME.

—Placido Domingo

She gave me great advice. She said that we had to acknowledge that we would never change our parents; we would have to change.

She welcomed me into her home, wherever that home was, unannounced, and always had something wonderful to eat. I can't use the word generous enough. She was generous with her time, her talents, her love, her acceptance, her wisdom, her spirit.

I was visiting her once with my boss from Appalachian State, and she offered me a bloody Mary on a Sunday morning after I had spent a particularly rowdy night before. My boss, who was the vice chancellor at ASU, told her I couldn't have a drink, and she told him that I was an adult and didn't need him to make decisions for me. That could be the first time I had permission to be an adult.

When I introduced family or friends to her, they immediately recognized a magical spirit and she became their friend too. It was wonderful to have this expanding family because of our connections to her.

Rosemary was one of those friends. One time, Mary Alice outfitted Rosemary and me for the Waterford Goddess Party (which she'd introduced me to a year earlier). We had long, flowing silk scarves and diaphanous garments and we carried a huge staff with a gold medallion on top. This was so we could make an entrance. At the last minute, Mary Alice told us she wasn't going, just us. It was an early version of what we dubbed the "Waterford exit." An especially tense example was when she turned her Waterford Fair chili party over to me right before dinner was to be served. She just left. She hated being the center of attention. Hated it. Yet she loved people and cooking for them and being with them.

We had many, many wonderful vacations at the farm with her. We sang and danced. Made art, took pictures, ate, cooked, drank, read poetry aloud. Read David Sedaris out loud. Played really loud music. Took outdoor showers. Listened to the rain and thunderstorms. Gossiped. Solved other people's problems. Solved our own problems. Did crossword puzzles. And laughed. A lot.

Be generous. Love with your heart wide open, whether for friends or their dogs or strangers. Capture the essence of the life around you and translate it into colors, into words, into gifts you can leave behind. **Paint your walls. Paint rocks and stones. Paint yourself. Be fully alive.** Leave a piece of yourself behind. Make art out of every day.

give yourself 10

Word: Who is the Mary Alice in your life? Describe their watchful generosity and spirit. How does it show up in the world?

Image: If you could paint a room in your house in any way you'd like, what would it look like? (What keeps you from doing that?)

give yourself 37

Seek ways to make your clothes, your house, your car a reflection of who *you* are. Each day, infuse your life with rich, vibrant color in some way. That might mean writing your favorite quotes on the wall (inside your closet, if you can't bring yourself to Sharpie up the living room). It might mean going through your closet once and for all to rid yourself of clothes that are "appropriate," but not "you."

Enjoy the little things, for one day you may look back and realize they were the big things. **—Robert Brault**

Do, or do not

Do, or do not. There is no try. —**Master Yoda**

Something floated to the surface of my consciousness recently, vying for frontal lobe space, squeezing into precious real estate needed for phone numbers, due dates for first-grade book reports, and the first verses of "The Love Song of J. Alfred Prufrock," which so often comes in handy at cocktail parties and auto repair shops.

What floated toward the light?

It was the concept of intention.

Suddenly I became aware of all those times I have responded to an invitation or a suggestion by saying "I'll try."

> "I'll try to make it to your party."
>
> "I'll try to be there at 4:00 p.m."
>
> "I'll try to get the papers graded by Monday."
>
> "I'll try to remember to send him a birthday card."
>
> "I'll try to write every day."
>
> "I'll try to get to the gym to train for my marathon."
>
> "I'll try to be a Nobel Peace Prize winner and I'll try to make my bed every day."
>
> "I'll try, I'll try, I'll try."

It suddenly occurred to me that this just wouldn't do. The answer was "yes" or "no," not "I'll try." Once I became aware of the slippery slope of "I'll try," **I realized that I've spent some fair amount of living in that between zone, neither a clear yes or a no, but a maybe.** And so have many others. Why, I wonder? Why so noncommittal? So we could hedge against disappointment (of ourselves and others)?

When I was chosen as an exchange student to Sri Lanka, it was a country I had never heard of. Once chosen, I heard the name everywhere. The same phenomenon occurred with "I'll try." Once I became aware of it, I heard it everywhere: "I'll try to get that in the mail today." "I'll try to visit you in intensive care." "I'll try to set up your iPod today."

No, my dear friend—you either will or you won't. There is no "try."

"I'll try" became the enemy of intention. And intention became important to me, as did direction.

I first realized the importance of intention and direction while teaching a course a few summers ago on "Imaginative Facilitation: East and West" with a friend and colleague from Tokyo, my brilliant friend Kichom Hayashi. A magical group of people had convened for our five-day course, one of whom was my business partner, David, who led us in a half-day workshop during the course using improv and theater techniques as a way to access the learning.

One exercise was something we affectionately called "Goats and Bananas," a nonsensical play of goofy lines and stage direction delivered to participants randomly on small strips of paper.

My direction, which started the play, was to walk to the center of the room and declare, "Goats and bananas!" Hence the name.

Another person held a slip of paper that read: "When someone says, 'Goats and bananas,' walk to the center of the room and chirp like a bird." And "When someone walks to the center of the room and chirps like a bird, stand on a chair and declare, 'Two can play that game!'" And "When someone stands on a chair and says, 'Two can play that game,' clap your hands and shout, 'Bravo! Bravo!'" And "When someone claps their hands and shouts, 'Bravo! Bravo!' skip around the room saying, 'Pop! Pop! Pop!'"

There was a part for everyone in the room, all connected and yet seemingly random and nonsensical. We laughingly delivered our lines, not knowing where this was headed. "Great job!" David said. We talked about our need to make sense of the random actions, develop cause and effect, look for linkages. But before too much intellectualizing, David exclaimed: "Let's do it again!" So off we went, goats and bananas!

"Superb!" he said. "Let's do it again, but exaggerate each action." So we did an opera version—bigger than life, hysterical even.

"Now let's add intention," he said. "When you deliver your line, I want you to deliver it with some intention—imagine you are trying to bewilder or seduce or alert or anger or comfort or pacify someone. Choose an intention and deliver your line to achieve that intention."

"Huh?" we all said collectively, but then we did it.

And **things changed—the tone, the nuance, the mood, the way in which we delivered our lines and interacted—it all changed.** The play changed. It was different, then, with intention—intention was powerful.

"Now," he said, "let's add direction—direct that intention to an Other in the room."

Wow.

The play became something altogether different, though those nonsensical lines remained the same. Intention and direction changed it, changed us. It was a physical knowing that we experienced, far beyond intellectualizing.

"Last time—direct your intention to the next in the sequence. No one is ever out of the play in this version," he directed. "Maintain the sequence, but engage from the first moment."

The deep, embodied, personal, gut understanding that emerged is hard to explain. Behind the laughter was a profound and compelling learning about intention and direction that has forced me to revisit my life to see how much intention and direction have, actually, been missing. Oh, sure, from the curriculum vitae, they appear front and center—sureness, direction, intention, accomplishment—it all appears to be there. But now I know differently—and rather than regret that the play could have been different, I have to work on making the next scenes different by being intentional, with direction.

We know there are sixteen ways to avoid saying "no" in Japanese. In the United States, "I'll try" is one of them. What's another? The ubiquitous "we'll see." Neither demonstrates much intention or direction, does it?

THERE ARE THREE WAYS TO LEARN ART: STUDY LIFE, PEOPLE AND NATURE. STUDY THE GREAT PAINTERS. PAINT.

—Irwin Greenberg

Remember goats and bananas. Add intention and direction to your life. Watch the play change in remarkable ways. Engage from the first moment. Do, or do not. There is no "try."

give yourself 10

Word: Choose. Get off the fence. Do it or not. Make bad art. You don't need a clean studio to do it. A woman named Kathleen recently told me of working with AIDS patients who were dying. Standing with her in one of the patient's rooms, a colleague asked if she wanted to go by "Kathy" or "Kathleen." As Kathleen demurred, citing the pros and cons of each name, the dying man struggled to raise himself up in his bed and said, "For God's sake, *choose*." What is one choice you are facing right now to which the dying man would have the same reaction?

Image: Draw the image of how it feels to say "yes" to that one choice. And draw an image of what saying "no" would feel like.

give yourself 37

Try to eliminate the word *try* from your vocabulary. I dare you.

The refusal to choose is a form of choice; disbelief is a form of belief.
—Frank X. Barron

Please lick the art

Art is a passion or it is nothing. —**Roger Fry**

Years ago, I sat at my kitchen table in Alexandria, Virginia, near George Washington's home, Mount Vernon. It was a Sunday, so I was reading *The Washington Post.* Perhaps we were even sitting outside on our small porch, tiled with what looked like non-vegan luncheon meats.

I was immediately struck by the desire to have had this idea myself: A writer had traveled around the country interviewing art museum guards about their favorite pieces of art in the museums they protected.

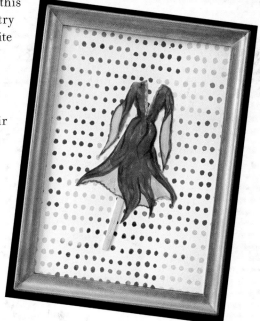

"Of course!" I said to John, excitedly. "Of course! Why didn't I think of this? It's perfect!"

I read with delight as stolid men and women in their starched museum guard uniforms relaxed into the question. Ignored by many museumgoers except as they represented the Rules, these guards all had ready answers—it was not a difficult question for them. Some were partial to the Masters, and would stand in front of them whenever possible as tourists flowed into galleries and back out. Some had requested to be stationed in the section of the museum with the impressionistic dots that had stolen their heart; others felt magnetically drawn to a particular cool iron sculpture in the garden or atrium.

When they talked about their special piece of art, they were more eloquent than a thousand art critics. Why? Because they didn't know—from an intellectual, critical place in their head—why they loved that particular still life or portrait or battle scene. They just *knew.* **They knew at a deeper level, at a place from the neck down, from their heart and soul and body, they knew.** The art moved them. It moved them. Not satisfied some epistemological, psychological gap in them, but *moved* them.

Passion should overwhelm reason time and again. —**Alvaro Castagnet**

My God, it was glorious. Reading that article was like seeing again for the first time, dissolving all the intellectual jargon I've ever heard about the form and function of a painting, and just leaning back into the comfy chair of recognition, identification, love.

What is it to be so drawn to a piece of work that you identify with it, that you have no words for it, that you cannot explain why you love it? What a glorious feeling. What art does that to you?

The Minneapolis Institute of Arts has a new T-shirt in its gift shop—with a story behind it, following a young fan's recent visit to the museum. In the museum's Gallery 308, museum guard Tim Piowtrowski noticed a little girl admiring a seventeenth-century portrait of French aristocrat Catherine Coustard by the painter Nicolas de Largillière. The little girl was so enamored of the dark blue velvet dress worn by the marquise in the painting that Mr. Piowtrowski had to admonish her: "Please don't lick the art," he said. That phrase now adorns a T-shirt on sale at the museum for $22.50. The painting was unharmed.

We need to lick more art, I'm thinking. Or be so passionately in love with it that we want desperately to lick it. Or so identify with it that we yearn to have created it ourselves.

WESTERN ART IS BUILT ON THE BIOGRAPHICAL PASSION OF ONE ARTIST FOR ANOTHER.

—Jim Dine

In the past few years, for example, I'm proud to report I have written several quite successful books under my pen name, Anne Lamott.

Okay, I lied.

I just *wish* I had written those books. Sometimes when I read them again and again, I even *believe* I have written them—like that weird thing that happens when you write a word like *suppose* or *nostril* or *petulant* over and over and over again until it becomes something unknowable, like you've made up a whole new word all by your lonesome. Well, it's sort of like that.

The one I most wish I had written is *Bird by Bird*. If the truth be told, and I guess now it will be, I carry my beloved hardback copy of *Bird by Bird* around with my own photograph pasted on the back of it, as if I myself, my little person, this one, had written it. (And it's an old photo, the kind that when you use it to announce your speech in a conference program, people act puzzled and disappointed when they finally meet you because, truthfully, you no longer look anything like that younger version of yourself, what with the prematurely gray hair and all . . .)

I read *Bird by Bird* several times a year, particularly in those moments when I think I should be writing, but am doubtful that I actually can, or when I'm in need of a reminder about what it means to write (not what it means to appear as a delightfully witty, thin, best-selling author on Oprah with good hair and eyebrows and a nifty bohemian chic outfit that you've designed and sewn yourself and that starts a fashion stampede, but, rather, what it means to actually sit down every morning and write, remembering Gene Fowler's somber acknowledgment that "writing is easy. All you do is stare at a blank sheet of paper until drops of blood form on your forehead").

In moments of sheer identification with what she's saying, I guess I *do* believe I've written *Bird by Bird,* the connection between her words and my thoughts is so close. Kind of like licking a piece of art in a museum. Or like reading Book 3 of *War and Peace,* that part where a soldier looks at the man who is about to execute him and says, "But you can't do this because you have no idea what my life means to me." *Yes! That's exactly it!* you think to yourself. Or reading that essay about having a fear of heights where the writer finally surfaces what your *own* fear of heights is all about, but which you had never known or articulated for yourself, even through all those years of watching the Fourth of July fireworks from the flat-roof-with-no-discernible-edge of your Capitol Hill house: "It's not a fear of falling, but a fear of flinging yourself off."

Lest you believe me insane, the idea of plastering your own photograph onto a book with which you so closely identify is a fantastic and poignant image from what I consider to be the Greatest American Novel and not just because I spent many tortured months writing my thesis on it—*The Recognitions* by William Gaddis. A head-on masterpiece, it is a complex and spectacular work about the simple distinctions between real and authentic, between faiths and fakes. Its theme is, shockingly, recognitions. On many levels, people and artists in the book identify and recognize themselves in others; **they hear their story in the voice of others, the way we sometimes meet someone and know that there is a connection there, unspoken and perhaps indefinable, but there,** as if we were standing on a balcony looking down and recognizing people on the ground below with whom we share some indefinable something. In it, among other moments of identification and recognition, a man carries around a book by Dostoevski with his own photograph pasted onto the back of it, calling into question the very concept of real and serving as the model for my own appropriation of *Bird by Bird.* Whew, that's a mouthful.

THERE ARE TWO TYPES OF PEOPLE IN THE WORLD: PEOPLE WHO ARE PASSIONATE ABOUT THINGS, AND PEOPLE WHO'VE HAD THEIR PASSION PUNCHED, BEATEN, OR WHATEVER OUT OF THEM.

—Kevyn Aucoin

That moment of recognition, identification. Reading something that so articulates what you believe and even what you didn't realize you believed. WANTING TO LICK THAT PAINTING. It's a magical moment, that. It's how I feel when I read Rilke telling me that I must change my life, when I watch Atticus Finch and Scout, when I first read *Ellen Foster,* or when I hear someone read the hot music of *Under the Volcano* to me in a slow, languid, southern voice. Or that odd feeling I had when I saw the movie *Slingblade,* my husband John recognizing it immediately when the lights in the theater came up: "That was the movie you were supposed to write, wasn't it?" he asked magically, right on target as usual.

First, find your book, the one you wrote (or, okay, the one you wish you had written, that special one in which you recognize your own thoughts coming back to you with a certain majesty) and paste your photograph on the back of it with abandon. **Find that painting that makes your heart soar.** Print out a copy of it and carry it in your wallet or hang it above your computer screen in your cubicle. Find the art you are so drawn to that licking it seems the logical next step.

give yourself 10

Word: Imagine a piece of art you love, one that you want to bump up against, get close enough to lick—what is that artwork or book of poems that brings out that impulse in you? Can you say why and how it has this impact on you? Try to articulate the impact. How does it make you feel?

Image: Create an image of that with yourself in it somehow—perhaps not a replica but something evocative of the piece (whether simply a color or the composition of the piece).

give yourself 37

Get close to something or someone—give yourself over. With this kind of passion comes vulnerability; you know that. Make note of the hesitations you have—what resistance do you have to licking the art? Is it that you need permission? From whom? What would happen if you asked for forgiveness, not permission? Notice your impulse for 37 days. Write about what it feels like to follow your impulse.

> Passion is universal humanity. Without it religion, history, romance and art would be useless.
> —**Honoré de Balzac**

Carry your own tuba

One person with passion is better than forty people merely interested.

—E. M. Forster

When I was in the sixth grade, as soon as I was eligible, I joined the band.

Girls played flute and clarinet, and boys played trombone and trumpet in those ancient days, long before sliced bread or ballpoint pens were invented and back when Chicken Pot Pies were New! As Seen on TV! Freeing Moms Everywhere from the Drudgery of Cookery!

Mr. Smith, our band director, would likely have passed a gallstone at the very idea of a *girl* in the low brass section. No, no, it just wouldn't do. And so we stuck to our reed instruments, longing for the day in eighth grade when we could break loose and switch to bass clarinet or the fantastically nasal oboe or the beautiful red bassoon.

Fast-forward several hundred years to my daughter Emma's entry into the sixth-grade band a few years ago. "Flute is nice," I said. "And very compact! Easy to transport! You could carry it home in your purple camouflage backpack!" My whole strategy to convince a twelve-year-old was evidently based on exclamation points.

"Nah," she said. "I think I'd like to play the trombone."

And then I said it, like that little boy in *A Christmas Story* when the lug nuts from the car tire go flying through the air as his dad is trying to change a flat, and the boy says, in very slow motion, something akin to "fudge": "But trombones are so heavy! Girls don't play trombone!" I heard myself say.

She turned to look at me, astonished at what she was hearing after all those evenings of captivity when I pulled out the flip chart and Mr. Sketch markers to explain what cultural norms and stereotypes were.

"What?" she asked. "Girls don't do what, exactly?"

"Just kidding," I said, realizing that my gender norms were showing, unable to believe what I had just said. Where did that come from? **How unconscious and deep-seated some of our beliefs about normalcy are.** "But flutes are so much lighter! Don't you think trombones are awfully heavy? And loud?" This from a woman who decades before had played Pee Wee football, the carrot-top who beat the boys in the sixth-grade softball toss.

I'll admit it—at this point I was in survival mode. Mid-forties, pregnant, new town. Emma was starting band just before I was due to give birth. Screaming infant and trombone. Screaming infant and trombone. Screaming infant and trombone. Call me crazy, but it did not appear to be a match made in heaven.

> TO STUDY MUSIC, WE MUST LEARN THE RULES. TO CREATE MUSIC, WE MUST FORGET THEM.
>
> —Nadia Boulanger

The sixth-grade band tryouts were an interesting ritual. Kids are called up one by one to blow in different mouthpieces, the band director makes a pronouncement, and their fates are sealed. If Emma had squeaked a pitiful little squeak in the trombone mouthpiece, her whole band history would be different.

But she didn't. Shy Emma took to the stage and ripped open a sound that stopped all noise in the band room. Fathers and mothers turned to look, the band director clapped her hands together in surprise and joy, and I dropped my Luna Bar but was too pregnant to bend over and pick it up.

"Wow!" the band director exclaimed. "That's impressive! LOW BRASS for you, young lady!"

Emma bowed her head, beaming.

Trombone it was. Turns out that everyone who heard her play talked about what a beautiful, unusual tone she had. The girl was born to play trombone. Until a year later when she was born to play tuba.

"Are you the only girl trombone player?" I asked after the first day of band. She rolled her eyes.

"Of course not, Mommm."

Of course not.

She joined the marching band in high school, sticking with it after a lot of her friends dropped out, a loyalty I first admired in middle school when she stuck with softball on a team that in two seasons got on base twice, and one of those was when Emma was hit by a ball thrown by a thirteen-year-old pitcher with obvious anger control issues and a strong fastball.

> THE FIELD OF CREATIVITY THAT EXISTS WITHIN EACH INDIVIDUAL IS FREED BY MOVING OUT OF IDEAS OF WRONG-DOING OR RIGHT-DOING.
>
> —Angeles Arrien

Tuba players switch to sousaphones for marching season, those big silver bells sitting atop their heads, seen from great distances on the field. Emma is a Very Serious Marcher. No joking around for her, eyes forward, back straight, dedication, deep bass sound. She is a force to be reckoned with on field at halftime, moving swiftly and surely into formation, an anchor of sound for the band to center itself around.

Have I mentioned once or twice or several hundred dozen times how much I love and respect her?

Turns out that girls do play trombone. And tuba. And sousaphone. And they become astronauts and astronomers and run for president and hopefully, one day, they will learn to become great, not just good—but great in their own private, personal definition of *great,* not society's. Hopefully one day the generation that has been told they can do anything, will—not because

they feel they need to measure up, or be a role model for their gender, or because that's the only way they can gain respect, but because they are following their passion, they *want* to, because they simply love the sound of low brass. Hopefully one day those who don't remember the days of Old Math (trombones = boys and flutes = girls) will realize that sometimes change starts with a tuba.

If you must have a rule to follow, I would suggest cultivating a dialogue with your inner voice . . . If you listen to the clues your own images offer, the resulting work will be fresh, and authentic. Fall in love with your world . . .
—**Jane Fulton Alt**

Your creative challenge

It is too easy to give up what you really want to do because nobody else who looks like you is doing it. Imagine the first men who entered nursing, the first male kindergarten teachers, the first women who busted out of woodwinds into low brass. Do what you love. March like you've never marched before, head held high, shoulders carrying that tuba.

give yourself 10

Word: What messages did you get as a child about what boys could do, or what girls could do? For example, Emma was once told she couldn't like Spider-Man because only boys like Spider-Man. (Cough.) List any such messages you have received in your life.

Image: What is your tuba or sousaphone? Create an image of your "tuba" with any language that comes to you in seeing it, holding it, wearing it now that you're able to.

give yourself 37

Pick one or two of the messages you wrote about on your card and spend these 37 days picking up that thing you were forbidden to do. Play with it, try it on for size, see what happens. Write every day for five minutes about what you are discovering about the "rules."

Jump your mask off

Speech was given to man to disguise his thoughts. —**Charles M. de Talleyrand**

I'm thinking that the human race needs to jump more.

And I'd add something to Mr. de Talleyrand's thought, above. Not only speech but also gravity disguises man's thoughts.

Last night my husband—the marvelous and eclectic and über-well-read John—handed me one of his favorite books, one I had long seen on our shelves but never read, with its distinctive red and cream and black cover encased in a wonderful thick transparent dust jacket.

I read it just before going to sleep and decided that in addition to dancing in my car more, I need to jump more, leap, evade gravity, go real. And I need to see other people jump more, too.

Ah, welcome to the fine art of Jumpology, sardonically outlined by famous photographer Philippe Halsman in this remarkable and odd and funny little book.

Halsman was a famous photographer with 101 *Life* magazine covers to his credit when he died in 1979. Chosen as one of the world's ten great photographers in an international poll, he was a recorder of the famous, creating iconic photos of Einstein, Dalí, Marilyn Monroe, and many more. Halsman felt a portrait that did not show psychological insight was "an empty likeness" of its subject.

On a routine assignment he discovered a technique that allowed him to go deeper in creating psychological portraiture. It all happened when the Ford Motor Company commissioned an official family photograph in honor of the company's fiftieth anniversary. After a long, tiring session with nine edgy adults and eleven restless children, he remembers that "there was the charming matriarch of one of the great American families, and suddenly, like a pang, I felt the burning desire to photograph her jumping."

Odder urges have occurred, I'm sure.

"May I take a picture of you jumping?" he asked Mrs. Edsel Ford. "I have never seen an expression of greater astonishment," he recalled. The astonished Mrs. Ford replied, "You want me to jump with my high heels?" She asked her children to excuse her and went with Halsman to the hall where she, indeed, jumped—having taken off those heels.

Next, her daughter-in-law, Mrs. Henry Ford II, requested a turn.

"I realized," Halsman wrote, "**that deep underneath people wanted to jump** and considered jumping fun."

Rolleiflex in hand and tongue in cheek, he invented his own Rorschach test—"jumpology"—and convinced his subjects to become airborne in the interest of science.

The "jump" pictures had charm, and over the next six years Halsman asked clients to jump for him. Van Cliburn, Edward R. Murrow, and Herbert Hoover declined, but most jumped, like the carefully buoyant Vice President Richard Nixon who jumped for Halsman in the White House.

Halsman claimed the jumps revealed character that was otherwise hidden. "When you ask a person to jump, his attention is mostly directed toward the act of jumping and the mask falls so that the real person appears."

Psychologists, he notes, have many methods for finding out what's behind our masks—psychoanalysis, hypnotism, Rorschach tests, associations tests, a battery of methods to which Halsman amusedly adds jumpology. He "analyzes" the photographs, commenting on his interpretation of jumps—the symbolism of the leg and arm positions, the face, the ways in which American jumps differ from British jumps. A new measure of cultural difference, imagine! Are your arms straight out, straight up? Your fists clenched or spread wide? Your knees straight or bent? Your mouth open or closed? (Halsman wasn't fooled by Tallulah Bankhead, who pretended to jump but kept one foot firmly on the ground—do I ever do that?) The corporate presidents who appear in the book, for example, all jumped exactly the same way—straight

It's great to be great, but it's greater to be human. —Will Rogers

legs, outstretched bent arms. The reporters were also in identical jump positions, stick figures straight with arms at their sides. Does our jump form determine our career, our destiny, our way of being in the world? He mused: "In a jump the subject, in a sudden burst of energy, overcomes gravity. He cannot simultaneously control his expressions, his facial and his limb muscles. The mask falls. The real self becomes visible. One has only to snap it with the camera."

Of course, knowing that the jump reveals one's character influences the jump, doesn't it? Marilyn Monroe's first jumps were like a free and exuberant girl on a playground. After Halsman indicated that jumps reveal character, she was unable to continue, paralyzed by the vulnerability.

What does my jump look like? To my critical eye, it's too constrained, too planned, too tight, too self-conscious, not like Oppenheimer fully extended and reaching the stars. I want to change that. I want mine to be more like a child's—unburdened by the observations of others, unplanned and full of sheer delight at being airborne—how miraculous! how unbelievable! how freeing! how carefree!

Halsman knew that we all try desperately to establish our identity. "This fascination with the human face has never left me . . . **Every face I see seems to hide and sometimes, fleetingly, to reveal the mystery of another human being** . . . capturing this revelation became the goal and passion of my life."

As Charles M. de Talleyrand said, language is a mask. In my training work, we know that using language is a way of being clever, of deflecting the truth, of masking; we must take language away when possible, to avoid that social masking, to get away from merely saying what Teacher wants, to get to our own truth, a truth that more often than not comes out in the body, not the brain. Escaping gravity takes away cleverness, leaving us with our glorious ordinary, our jump.

Forget Myers-Briggs personality type tests and Rorschach assessments—how do you jump? **Examine your
psychological portraiture in midair, without gravity
to hide behind.** Jump! Jump alone. Jump with friends.
Jump with your whole damned management team.
And ask someone (a friend, a stranger on the street)
to take a photo so you can examine your portrait in
midair. In what ways does it illustrate You, that real
You without the social mask, that You not bound
by gravity, the You of the group? Remember: Deep
underneath, people want to jump.

give yourself 10

Word: When's the last time you jumped? Now do
the unexpected and jump. What's *your* version of jump? What keeps you
from jumping?

Image: What do you look like when you've left behind your mask? When
you've left the earth in mid-jump? Create an image of you jumping.

give yourself 37

How could you surprise yourself every day? Speak with an accent, eat dessert
first, wear two different shoes? For 37 days try to let go of the rules and leave
gravity behind. Do one thing each day that is counterintuitive for you. See
what your "mask" looks like unadorned.

> I'D RATHER TEACH ONE BIRD TO SING THAN
> TEN THOUSAND STARS HOW NOT TO DANCE.
>
> —e. e. cummings

reluctant poet

You could be writing about the new garden. Now there's a metaphor
you could chew on for hours, if your mind was in it. But alas,
today you are a reluctant poet, seeing the dahlia on your
back deck simply as a dahlia, and the basil plant as nothing else
than a fledgling herb nestled next to sweet spearmint. Today,
you ate French toast, watched television, spoke to a friend
who called to say hello, rinsed dishes, contemplated laundry,
decided against it, sat on your stone-grey couch to send
an email or two. Nothing mythic here at all, no magic in the least.
And yet how ripe this nothing of a peach, how filling this plain feast.

—Maya Stein

CHAPTER EIGHT

Clear Ground: *Stop Trying So Hard*

*If the desire to write is not accompanied by actual writing,
then the desire must be not to write.* —**Hugh Prather**

I started my blog, 37days, on January 3, 2005. It is the best job I never had.

It began as a simple promise to myself.

For years I made the usual New Year's
resolutions, including the one about writing every day, and yet for years I had to face
the emptiness of those resolutions gone
to envy, sometimes just a few weeks into a
new year—all those journals stepped into
and impossible to continue with so many
days missing, the regret at the gaps too
large to overcome, the "I'll try," not "I will."

Create spaciousness
so creativity can breathe.
Give up your perfectionism.
Stop comparing yourself with others.
Make many mistakes.
Make many paintings.

Evidently those promises to myself were
not enough to keep the pen moving—or
maybe the desire wasn't really to write, but
to complain about not having the time or
space or perfect conditions for writing. Or
perhaps I hadn't yet found the voice, the
impetus for voice, or the place to stand while telling the story.

Serendipitously (as most things are), at a writers' conference around that
same time, I took a most meaningful class taught by Sebastian Matthews, a
poet and memoirist. Sometimes what we need to hear is right in front of us.
Scheduled to take a different course during that hour, instead I found myself

sitting in a circle of writers in his workshop, hearing what I needed to hear: his clarifying and compelling voice expressing the framing for these words, this writing, the work I had already begun unknowingly.

In fact, his voice and way of being in the world mirrored exquisitely the force behind these words this year—a meeting of pen and paper that could not have happened before, so perhaps I shouldn't rue its delay. "What is your occasion for speech?" he quietly asked the circle of bodies around him, the first in a series of provocative questions he asked us to consider:

Who am I to tell this story?

What is my occasion for speech?

Where do I stand telling this story?

What ground do I need to clear?

"Walk into the threshold of the story you're already telling," he said. "Write about what you see. The reason for the telling is the story. **We talk about needing to find our voice, but it's not missing—it's just sometimes inaccessible.**"

There is a spaciousness that is needed for creativity. How are you creating spaciousness in your life?

Examine your occasion for speech. Situate yourself in time and place. Clear your own ground.

> When you look at art made by other people, you see what you need to see in it.
> —**Alberto Giacometti**

Shave with Ockham's razor

Everything should be made as simple as possible, but not simpler.

—**Albert Einstein**

In the summer of 1996, I had a bout of terrible headaches—debilitating, numbing, paralyzing brain crushers. I was convinced they were symptoms of a brain tumor; John quietly suggested that it might be a vitamin deficiency.

In fact, they were something in between brain tumor and vitamin deficiency—migraines—and were mainly solved by quitting my job. Not that they were stress-related or anything. Ahem.

To me, my headaches are always Intracranial Aneurysms, sore shoulders are a harbinger of Ewing's Sarcoma, indigestion is a Massive Myocardial Infarction, to which John replies: "Vitamin deficiency. Vitamin deficiency. Vitamin deficiency."

More often than I'd like to admit, I assume the complex, the catastrophic, while John always opts for the simplest explanation possible—"Eat more carrots or arugula or drink more water or take vitamin C and you'll be fine," he'll say. He's always right.

So when he told me the story of Kevin Mench this week, I had to smile.

First, let me admit that I like baseball (though I had never heard of Kevin Mench). My baseball heyday was years ago when I kept up with the New York Yankees, in the day of Don Mattingly, then in the era of the beautiful Andy Pettitte (before he became the cheating Andy Pettitte) and the idiosyncratic Chuck Knoblauch—I loved Knoblauch's obsessive-compulsive habit of ripping open the Velcro on his batting gloves, then closing the straps quickly, then ripping them open again and closing them quickly six times before each pitch, accompanied by that odd spring-loaded knee-bend, butt stuck straight out, those squinted eyes and lips pushed forward that characterized his batting stance.

I was saddened when, all of a sudden, Chuck lost the ability to throw to first base: He would freeze, overthrow, underthrow, badly throw—a failure that finally took him from second base to left field to out of the game altogether.

I miss his intensity on the field. I wonder what deep-seated psychological issues kept him from throwing to first base? Or perhaps it was just a vitamin deficiency?

Outfielder Kevin Mench wasn't doing so well, either, one year. He was in his fifth season with the Texas Rangers, and was coming off consecutive twenty-five-homer years. In a game against the Los Angeles Angels, he had become one of only seven players to homer in three consecutive innings. Then the homers stopped. He was in a slump and, finally, unable to play.

What happened? The batting coaches were consulted. Elaborate investigations were undertaken, to no avail—he still wasn't hitting. Further study ensued, teeth were gnashed, batting practices were taped and watched, doctors were called.

Finally he happened to mention that his foot hurt. Turns out, his shoes were too little.

He had been wearing size 12 shoes since he was fifteen years old, but it was time for a bigger shoe.

Mench started hitting home runs right after he got his new size 12½ shoes. Just a half size larger and he's hitting the ball again. He was soon on a streak—a Texas Rangers record with home runs in six straight games, including two grand slams, and twenty RBIs in a week.

"I'm thinking about changing shoes, too," teammate Gerald Laird said at the time.

"I'm hoping next year he goes to 13s," manager Buck Showalter joked.

Mench is only the fourth player in the past thirty years with twenty RBIs in seven games, joining Sammy Sosa (twenty-two in 2002), Albert Belle (twenty-one in 2000), and Mattingly (twenty in 1987). It only took a half-size larger shoe.

Ockham's razor is a logical principle attributed to the medieval philosopher William of Ockham, a principle stating that one should not make more assumptions than the minimum needed. It's often called the "principle of parsimony," usually interpreted to mean something like "the simpler the explanation, the better" or "don't multiply hypotheses unnecessarily." It underlies all scientific modeling and theory-building, admonishing us to choose the simplest from a set of otherwise equivalent models of possible solutions. In any given model, Ockham's razor helps us to "shave off" those concepts, variables, or constructs that are not really needed to explain the phenomenon.

> You can paint an entire painting with one stroke.
> —Quang Ho

Contrary to popular belief, Ockham doesn't assert that the simpler explanation is always more correct or that the more complex explanation is always less correct.

Rather, **the point is to start from the simplest possible explanation and only make it more complex when absolutely necessary—rather than the other way around**, which is tempting, isn't it? Brain tumor is infinitely more interesting than vitamin deficiency; deep-seated psychological obstacle more intriguing than too-small shoes . . .

Ockham insisted that valid, reasonable explanations had to be based upon simple, observable facts, supplemented by logic. Many scientists have adopted or reinvented Ockham's razor, as in Leibniz's "identity of observables" and Isaac Newton's rule: "We are to admit no more causes of natural things than such as are both true and sufficient to explain their appearances."

The most useful statement of the principle for scientists is, "If you have two theories that both explain the observed facts, then you should use the simpler until more evidence comes along." Or, "The simplest explanation for some phenomenon is more likely to be accurate than more complicated explanations." Or, "If you have two equally likely solutions to a problem, pick the simplest." Or, "The explanation requiring the fewest assumptions is most likely to be correct." Or perhaps I should follow the principle of Ockham's razor and simply say, "The simpler the better."

This principle goes back at least as far as Aristotle, who wrote, "Nature operates in the shortest way possible." The final word is often attributed to Einstein, himself a master of the quotable one-liner: "Everything should be made as simple as possible, but not simpler."

How difficult it is to be simple. —Vincent van Gogh

After the *Challenger* explosion, one of the century's great physicists, Richard Feynman, was on the commission investigating the disaster. During the hearings, many engineers and scientists testified exhaustively on their findings about the composition and construction of the O-rings on the *Challenger*, to no conclusive finding. This went on for some time, until one day Feynman took a model of the O-ring, put it into his glass of ice water, left it momentarily, then extracted it and shattered it on the table, demonstrating the failure in the O-rings due to freezing temperatures in Florida at launch time, leading to the terrible tragedy in 1986. **Sometimes simple works.**

When I was in graduate school at the University of Virginia in the mid-1980s, I awoke one morning to a nauseating, powerful headache, one that scared me, with a feeling that a steel pipe was jammed from my spine into my head. My friend Haynes kept popping in to make sure I was okay; I wasn't. I called my mother. She called back every few hours with a new diagnosis: "I talked to Lexine and she said Uncle Homer's daughter's boyfriend's sister's husband had Rocky Mountain spotted fever and he had exactly the same symptoms; get to the emergency room." Just as I would drift off to sleep, she would call back: "Remember when Troy Dobson's wife's sister's husband's aunt Jessie's boy contracted spinal meningitis? It sounds like what you have; go to the emergency room." Hours later, another call, another diagnosis. I must admit, I was worried, too.

So I did go to the emergency room and I was immediately hospitalized. Three days later, after tests for Rocky Mountain spotted fever, multiple sclerosis, spinal meningitis, and several hundred other dire diseases, Dr. Steven Meixel from student health (The Best Doctor in the World) arrived on the scene and asked me some very simple questions: "Did anything about your diet change? Did you start eating anything just before this started? Did you stop eating anything just before this started? Did you run out of anything that you usually eat, for example?"

I had run out of coffee the day before the headache started.

It was caffeine withdrawal. Plain and simple.

I miss Chuck Knoblauch. I wish he had tried bigger shoes, or maybe batting gloves with less Velcro.

As Alfred North Whitehead has said, "Simple solutions seldom are. It takes a very unusual mind to undertake analysis of the obvious."

I wonder what simple solutions I'm overlooking. What is keeping me from throwing to first, from hitting home runs, from analyzing the obvious . . . ?

I think I'll check my shoe size. Maybe that's the problem. Maybe it's not the earth's rotational pull multiplied by the weight of water plus pi squared or some equally difficult algorithm, but just the size of my shoes that's the problem. **Maybe it's something simple that's keeping me from moving forward, not something complex.** Maybe it's just a vitamin deficiency, dehydration, too-small shoes, or running out of coffee. Maybe it's simple, not hard. Maybe it's not complex and convoluted and difficult, but easy.

Wear bigger shoes. Even a half size larger might make all the difference.

Shave with Ockham razor; go for simple explanations first. (Of course, the corollary to Ockham's razor is Hanlon's razor: "Never attribute to malice that which can be adequately explained by stupidity.")

give yourself 10

Word: Notice your first thought about a problem facing you, and work on the second. So if you often go straight to complicated solutions, go simpler. What's the essential piece? What can you eliminate?

Image: Draw a legal pad on your index card. Write two phrases on it to represent what you must do or you will die. Just two.

give yourself 37

Be less fancy. Look around and simplify. Declutter: simplify the field of vision in your house, every day for 37 days.

> LIFE IS SIMPLIFIED WHEN THERE IS ONE CENTER; ONE REASON, ONE MOTIVATION, ONE DIRECTION AND PURPOSE.
>
> —Jean Fleming

Sit down and write

A writer writes. A painter paints. —**Tom McKenzie**

I get a lot of e-mails from people asking how to write (a book). So I thought outlining my thoughts on the topic might be helpful—to me, in order to clarify the thoughts I have about writing—and, perhaps, to others. (You don't write? Substitute *paint, embroider, sing, knit, parent . . .* for the word *write.*)

1. Don't set out to write a book.

Form is not content. Let's say that again: FORM IS NOT CONTENT. A book is nothing more than a commodification of ideas. Start with the ideas, the emotions, the thing you most long to say. If you don't know, the writing itself will help surface what it is you want to say, but **sitting still and waiting for a book to spring fully formed from your forehead will never happen.** Will. Never. Happen. Listening to what other people have to say also won't help. Good God, no wonder we all have writer's block. We're not even writing. Plumbers don't have plumber's block, do they? *No, they get on the floor and clear out the Windex and evidence of mouse poop under the sink and get to plumbing;* which leads me to point number 2.

2. Sit the hell down and write.

Writer Ron Carlson has written so eloquently about this in his book *Ron Carlson Writes a Story.* He reminds us to sit back down and stay in the room. When everything else in the world seems more attractive than actually sitting down and putting pen to paper (how sweetly archaic I am, thinking *anyone* actually writes on a college-ruled legal pad with a fountain pen anymore besides me), sit back down and stay in the room. Sure, I know the laundry just got fascinating, but sit the hell down and write.

3. Write to write.

Don't say you're a writer if you're not writing. You're not a writer, and who cares anyway, if you're not writing. Even if you're writing, don't call yourself a writer. Say, instead, "I write." It's the verb that's important, not the noun.

"I haven't been able to write," people say to me all the time. "No, actually," I respond, "you *have* been able to write, but you have chosen not to." They usually walk away unhappy. We are always—*always*—in choice. If you have a napkin and a pencil nub or a piece of dirt on a stick, you can write. Don't let the "writer" take precedence over the "writing." Let go of outcome. Forget blog statistics and the endless "freebies" that have sprouted online. Why does your blog need to lead anywhere? What's all this striving about? Don't search endlessly for a book deal before you've even written anything. Go back to number 2: Sit the hell down and write. Sit alone with yourself and a piece of paper without thinking about an audience, your database, the best way to market using social media.

4. Long to say something.

"How can I build a successful blog?" people ask me. I do not have a clue. I do everything wrong—my posts are too infrequent and far too long for a nation shocked by long uninterrupted blocks of text. What is your intention? To build a successful blog, or **to actually say what is inside your heart and mind and every single bloody cell of your being, and that you must somehow export it out into the world before you die?** Much writing I read these days is to sell something by a formula. Is that your highest purpose? Is that the voice that is dying to be let free into the world? If it is, great, that's fantastic! If not, stop it. Stop it. Sit with yourself and your unique place in the world and write it all down. Write it all down. Speak your voice. So many people say they need to find their voice. You *have* a voice, now use it, damn it. In the writing comes the thread. In the writing comes your unique voice, your way, your sense-making of the world around you. Can't say what you want because people won't understand or like it? Who are you living for? Yourself or people with wallets? Yourself or applause? Yourself or validation?

5. Name the direction of your intention.

See number 4, above. Why are you doing this? Why do you want to write? To be on a best-seller list or to say something that only you can say in the way that you can say it? To leave behind a record of having been here? To scratch out some small surface of your story for others to learn from? To tell your Truth as only you can see it? To get optioned for a movie? To enroll people on your precious database, like so many prizes in a Cracker Jack box? Why? Name the direction of your intention. You can't play two intentions at a single time on stage—which are you playing? Are you warning Hamlet or getting the audience to love you? Warn Hamlet.

6. Ignore everybody.

"People won't like what I've written. They won't buy it. It'll never get published." WHO CARES? Who cares. Annie Dillard once said you have to be an orphan to write. Be an orphan. Write it. If you fear leaving it behind should you be hit by a large flock of seagulls and killed on your way to lunch, write it and fling it into the air by hitting DELETE. The only thing important about that difficult scene you need to write, but which would embarrass you if others read it, is that you wrote it. Write it all down, the worst imaginable things you think (trust me, you are not alone in enjoying the smell of your own farts). Just write it. Delete it if you must; the important part is to write it. Get it out of your system. Stop trying to manifest an audience.

7. The writing is everything.

Not the publishing. Not the work-shopping. Not the agent-shopping. Not the Amazon sales rank. Not the deciding who will play you in the movie (Meryl Streep, of course, for 90 percent of us, what with the accents and all). No, just the writing. The unsexy part. The part where blood drips from your forehead and you imagine yourself far more precious and special than you are.

8. Shut up about ideal conditions.

I am tired of hearing myself whine about needing a writing shed—and, frankly, I'm tired of hearing you whine about it, too. I have two words for you: Concentration Camp. Beautiful, haunting, exquisite music, art, and writing, were born of Auschwitz. Shut up about needing different-colored walls. These are all deflections that serve only to keep you from doing the work. Your studio is too messy? Clean it the hell out and get to work. You don't have a studio? Write at the dining room table like I do. Don't have a dining room? Sit on the toilet and write. Don't have a toilet? Got floor? Don't have time? Have a full-time job? So do I. So did William Gaddis, author of one of the most amazing American novels ever written. So did poet Wallace Stevens. Get over it. Talking about not having enough time takes up more time than it would take to actually write.

9. Don't believe the hype.

Write your heart out. Put it out into the world (or not) and then write more. Don't stop to head up your own parade. Just write. **Write like you are dying. You are.**

10. Read more.

Read like your hair is on fire.

11. Don't take one more class.

Everything you are doing to avoid actually writing is a deflection, including taking more classes. You know enough. Do you know the alphabet? Do you have a brain and a heart? You can write with JUST THAT KNOWLEDGE AND EQUIPMENT (see below).

12. Make do with the pen you have.

I've heard the excuses. If only I had one of those cool astronaut pens that write upside down and in the rain, then I could write the Great American Novel. If I had one of those weatherproof notebooks . . . See number 8. Write with a pencil nub. Just write. You don't have the latest studio equipment? Too bad. Pretend you're MacGyver and have to save the world with a safety pin and a piece of string. Imagine you are on a plane that is going down into the ocean and you need to scrawl last your words on a vomit bag with an eyeliner because that's all you can find and time is short. Use what you can find. Because time is short.

That is all. End of rant. For now.

See above. Do the work. And sometimes, as William Stafford says, "Lower your standards."

give yourself 10

Word: What's within reach of where you are sitting right now? Choose one object you can see near your left hand. Describe it.

Image: Draw what you have within reach to write with. Is it a pen? A pencil? A gold-encrusted Mont Blanc? A crayon? Good. Perfect! Pick it up. Now use it to write.

give yourself 37

Gather 37 small objects from your home and put them into a paper bag—don't think about them, just put them in. At the beginning of each day for the next 37 days, pick a small object from the paper bag, randomly. Write about it, describe it.

There's nothing to writing. All you do is sit down at a typewriter and open a vein.—Walter Wellesley "Red" Smith

Always yield to aircraft

My task is to make you hear, feel and see. That and no more, and that is everything.
—**Joseph Conrad**

I'm intimately familiar with the Cincinnati–Northern Kentucky International Airport. Franny in Laptop Lane greets me by name; the store Toto sells good greeting cards; Starbucks is near Gates 40–69; the restaurant near the information booth in Terminal C isn't worth waiting in line for; the blond-haired agent at Gate 56 is chronically mean-spirited, and even more so when it is raining, the barometric pressure is high, or it's a day of the week that ends with the letters *d-a-y*.

Last week I took the shuttle bus from Terminal A to Terminal C for my connecting flight, a trip usually done on autopilot: I roll my L.L. Bean Dark Green Medium Adventure Duffle with the Telescoping Handle and Smooth-Glide Wheels aboard the shuttle, stand looking at people and making up funny, yet poignant stories about their lives inside my head until they catch me looking, then disembark. This time, though, I paid attention to the trek. **I watched, trying to decipher the rhythm of the airfield, the ebb and flow,** the intricate dance of weary travelers across asphalt, all those service vehicles darting to and fro.

As we lumbered toward the terminal, I noticed all manner of messages painted right onto the ground, instructing shuttle bus drivers and baggage carts and little catering trucks carrying small vacuum-sealed packets of peanuts and not much else as they move around the airfield. There were the usual: STOP. RIGHT TURN ONLY. ONE WAY. Signs that reflect symbols that reflect commonly understood social rules of conduct, ways of being together in the world, making life predictable and safe.

But as I looked at the asphalt speeding under us, I saw a sign that made me laugh out loud, much to the surprise of my fellow strap-hangers intent on disengagement. The sign read, simply, YIELD TO AIRCRAFT.

Well, yes, indeedy, that sounds like mighty fine advice to me, I thought to myself as I smiled. *After all, who might win? A twenty-six-passenger shuttle bus or a 545,000-pound, 440-seat, 209-foot-long Boeing 777 aircraft?*

Yield to aircraft.

It seems obvious, doesn't it? Yet, like ubiquitous product warnings, perhaps it is there because someone didn't yield to aircraft. THIS LIQUID IS VERY HOT became standard reading on coffee cup lids because a woman dropped her coffee (to say it was hot is a tad redundant, don't you think?) in her lap at a McDonald's drive-through and sued (and worse yet, won); I hate to think what awful mouth-shrinking event resulted in DO NOT USE ORALLY being printed on each box of Preparation H hemorrhoid cream . . . but I digress.

I cocked my head to the side, en route to Terminal C. Yield to aircraft. Is it possible that this advice applies to life, too?

Slow down, look around, make sure there isn't a 545,000-pound, 440-seat, 209-foot-long Something bearing down on me. If there is, perhaps the best course of action is to yield to it, for goodness' sake; I can minimize the damage by not driving straight into its path. Perhaps I should take a little vacation in the islands until it passes on by, for example.

> [Truth has rough flavours
> if we bite it through.
> **—George Eliot**]

Obviously, there are times when fighting the 545,000-pound gorilla (inequity, discrimination, abuse, low-fat foods that are not really low-fat) is the only way, the right way, the hard but necessary way, the way that must be taken at any cost. But as I contemplated the wisdom of the sign, I realized that I've often moved into the path of an "aircraft" when yielding to it would have made more sense, when I didn't need to do that, when it was more hurtful to me than helpful to others, when slowing and yielding was the healthiest thing to do. Perhaps I even threw myself into the path of the "aircraft" so others could save me, or see me save myself. It's possible.

So that simple sign not only made me laugh; it got me to thinking about symbols, signs, paths of least resistance. And paths of *most* resistance, which are usually more apt to result in creative sparks.

Signs are all around us—can we see them, read them, understand them? Do we know that the signs we see are simply referential to reality, not reality itself?

You can observe a lot by just watching. —**Yogi Berra**

Perhaps obvious signs aren't obvious, like yielding to aircraft or STEEP DROP BEYOND WALL. You think?

Sometimes I see signs, but can't read them—like being in Hong Kong for the first time without Chinese-language skills, bewildered, lost, afraid—not knowing what even the simplest of signs meant, unable to place myself in a cultural, known context that would make sense to me. When I can't read the signs, I feel fearful and less myself; I pull myself in, I protect my ignorance, my confusion.

And sometimes there are just too many signs, like street posts in DC with fourteen signs, some seemingly contradictory, pointing to different places at the same time, regulating parking on alternate rainy Thursdays—too much to take in too quickly; again, **slowing down would help us read the signs and avoid a wrong turn, but everyone is honking, the pressure is too great, we speed past, straight into the path of the airplane.**

I see signs everywhere, in the smallest of glances; they point beyond themselves to something else. It is the "something else" that is important to me, that I want to find or see, that bears understanding.

As Paul Tillich said (won't Mel Keiser, my religion professor from Guilford College, be proud that I remembered Paul Tillich?), "The red sign at the street corner points to the order to stop the movements of cars at certain intervals. A red light and the stopping of cars have essentially no relation to each other, but conventionally they are united as long as the convention lasts. The same is true of letters and numbers and partly even words. They point beyond themselves to sounds and meanings."

And like words, symbols frame reality in a certain way, don't they? My word becomes my reality; I frame reality in a certain way by the signs and symbols I use and those I pay attention to—either positive and negative, either "yes, and" or "yes, but."

Years ago, I interviewed a young man who had created a new access symbol, changing the static wheelchair figure omnipresent in "handicapped" parking signs to something more fluid and active, an image featuring a person in a wheelchair moving through an open door. In so doing, he framed the chair as a tool for movement, the open door a symbol of possibility, rather than being closed down, bound by the chair, static and still. He reframed our feelings about people in wheelchairs in the process, and perhaps their own sense of themselves as well. Reframing the signs.

NOT MUCH CAN BE SEEN IN THE DARK, BUT SENSED YES.

—Joseph Tany

What if our street signs were different, I wonder? What if we found ourselves at the corner of Peace and Patience more often?

I read signs daily: the hydraulic system failing on a plane trip is a sign that I should stop working with the man traveling with me and change my life, recurring migraines are a sign that I should leave my job, a book featuring an essay about my dad arriving on the anniversary of his death is a sign that Daddy knows, that life is somehow more than arbitrary.

Or not.

Signs are my sense-making tools. They, like objects in my home, are referential to some meaning in me quite unrelated to the sign, the thing itself. I make meaning of them by making stories of them.

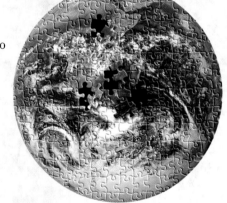

Read the daily signs; pay attention to the Big Ones; discard some. Sure, there will be some signs we miss; there will be others whose symbols and meaning we misread; there will be signs that we ignore—and there are signs that, honestly, aren't significant, not in the long term. Just don't ignore the big ones, the aircraft ones, the smoosh-you-into-the-runway ones. Pay attention to the signs around you—see them, read them, make meaning of your life through them, and yield to aircraft.

give yourself 10

Word: Your body is often the source of your most potent "sign." Migraines, unease, name your symptom. All might be giving us a sign. What aches do you feel? What is your body telling you?

Image: Draw the signs you see around you in daily life—not their meaning, just the signs themselves. What do they say? How many do you see in a day?

give yourself 37

Keep a Body Journal for 37 days on your index cards, perhaps with images on one side and words on the other. Note how you are feeling, physically and emotionally. I'd even track what you're eating and the exercise you're doing, for those 37 days. What is happening externally to you (what stresses or events)? Keep as detailed a picture as you can of the ways you are responding to external events—do you eat from hunger or emotion? Is your body warning you or advising you in some way? Use your index cards to create a written and visual journal of those 37 days. Discover what you discover. Some of what you discover might be those things that keep you out of your most creative spaces.

Everyone is in the best seat.

—John Cage

Be the storm's eye

For a long time it had seemed to me that life was about to begin—real life. But there was always some obstacle in the way. Something to be got through first, some unfinished business, time still to be served, a debt to be paid. Then life would begin. At last it dawned on me that these obstacles were my life. —**Alfred Souza**

I found that quote by Alfred Souza in the most-read magazine in my mother's house many, many years ago—way back in the 1980s, that wacky decade of my youth now depressingly the subject of retro parties on college campuses (retro! the nerve!).

Being quoted in the *Wall Street Journal, Financial Times, New York Times, Fortune* magazine—all that fluff and business blah-blah was *nothing* compared with the thrill for my mother when my name appeared in print in *Reader's Digest.*

"Aunt Estaleen showed it to me at the beauty shop, and there you were!" she fairly well yelled into the phone on the Big Day. "I called Uncle Charles to tell him and he just cried," she called back to say later. To merit two long-distance calls in one day, you know the *Reader's Digest* is big news in our family.

So way back in the 1980s, I did the absolute unthinkable when I found Souza's quote about life's obstacles in "Quotable Quotes" on one of those small pages near "Points to Ponder," "Life in These United States," "Day's Work," and "Humor in Uniform": I tore it out, a travesty, a Sin, an unforgivable selfishness.

Thinking fast, lest I be discovered disfiguring the Holy Grail, I slipped the wafer-thin page into my passport where it remained as I flew around the world, ostensibly speaking at conferences but really just meeting interesting people; doing the polka at an Australian hoedown with a brilliant British professor in his velvet smoking jacket; learning how to order beer in Serbian, Italian, Hebrew, and Czech; watching gorgeous sunsets over Wellington while eating delicious miniature stuffed pumpkins at the home of a high-ranking official in my Clearness Committee there; and forging lifelong friendships with Israeli tank commanders.

Every time I got on a flight, I found myself unfolding that page again, trying to remind myself that those flights weren't an obstacle, they were my life. Then I lost my passport in Asia, along with Daddy's last grocery list and Souza's quote, its wisdom misplaced for years.

En route from Oregon to North Carolina recently, while in an airport gift shop searching for the newest *People* magazine (for my continuing research on the epistemological and phenomenological assessment of core American values, yeah, that's it), I happened upon that favorite quote on a magnet. It was like finding an old friend, seeing that philosophy of life spelled out again.

What I've come to realize in the life I've lived since that inglorious moment of defacing my mother's *Reader's Digest* is how significantly and how powerfully we try to make life nice and neat, moving with surgical cleanness and methodical rapidity to our goals, feeling like everything that gets in the way (messy, messy) is just an obstacle rather than life itself, the process. That if we could get past these inconveniences and errands, if we could keep up with mowing the lawn, putting the new swing set together with its missing screws and bad instructions, cooking nightly dinners for our family, and getting the car inspected—if we could get past all that, then we could (if we just had that atelier in Paris or on a Greek island and a beautiful laptop with a 17-inch screen and one of those iPod nanos with a lovely, handcrafted wooden case on which to listen to Joan Armatrading full-volume while writing, and some significant amount of cash and good fountain pens and letterpress-printed stationery), then we could finally write that great American novel, solve world hunger, and get a poem published in *The New Yorker*. I mean really, have you seen some of those poems?

> The hardest thing about art is letting it be easy.
> **—Fern Kagan**

We have an urge to get past the messy, messy once and for all. To get to that point of clarity where the "obstacles" fall away: The desk is clear and there are no toddlers running around with diapers half off, no teenagers remembering at breakfast that they need to make a full-scale plaster model of the universe by tomorrow morning—to clear the decks and make nice, make everything clear and nice and uninterruptible. Yes! When we get there, we will indeed be recognized as a genius! Then our work in the world will be powerful! We will be on *Oprah*! Our ship will finally come in! We will save lives! We will miraculously be able to make a soufflé! We will know the difference between poison ivy and ivy, how to pronounce Csikszentmih- alyi's name, and fit into those jeans! All our plants will live and thrive, proving our mother-in-law wrong! If only all those pesky obstacles would go away.

> THINGS ARE NOT DIFFICULT TO MAKE; WHAT IS DIFFICULT IS PUTTING OURSELVES IN THE STATE OF MIND TO MAKE THEM.
>
> —Constantin Brancusi

When I worked on the Semester at Sea program, we hit rough weather (can you say typhoon?) three days into the ten-port, three-month voyage around the globe. As a result of significant damage to the ship, we were delayed going into several ports, which meant that in-country programs were altered or canceled altogether. "I want my money back," wailed one student. "We're missing trips and that's not fair," he went on. "This isn't the real Semester at Sea." (*No,* I thought to myself, *we weren't supposed to do emergency surgery in the lounge on Promenade Deck to reattach fingers after the storm, either, but tell that to those wayward digits.*). "Interesting perspective," I replied. "but this is *your* Semester at Sea. This is the one you have, the only one, yours. There isn't a more real one."

The more he measured his Semester at Sea against the ideal one—the four-color brochure one—the less content he was, missing in the meantime the experience of this real one, the one he was actually experiencing, this trip of a lifetime, his. The obstacles *were* his Semester at Sea. (And, I might add— just as a fairy tale becomes more interesting and engaging when bad things happen, just as Story needs Conflict to move forward, so too a four-month voyage at sea takes on an energy of its own when a typhoon provides the story spark. Talk about community-building . . . but I digress.)

The daily moments of decision and errands, all those trips to the grocery store and dry cleaners, those delayed and canceled flights, the seasons of cookie dough sales to raise money for the band, the messy desk and less-than-ideal writing conditions, all those nights on the road sleeping under depressing hotel art depicting Mount Vesuvius and Bad Apples—they are all my life, not obstacles. I need to own my typhoon.

What is your perfect storm, those obstacles to achieving your dreams? **Own your typhoon;** it isn't an obstacle, no. It's your life, that one wild and precious one, your only one, it. You're the eye of that storm. (And throw away the four-color brochure. Looking at it will only make you miss the real thing.)

give yourself 10

Word: What is your typhoon right now, that source of anxiety and pain and storminess?

Image: Create an image of the messiness of your life, not the perfect four-color brochure version. Own the messiness, the hot chaos. From that space comes art.

give yourself 37

Every day for 37 days, write, paint, create something that reflects a typhoon in your life, past or present. Walk into it, toward it, not away from it.

I'VE LEARNED THAT YOU CAN TELL A LOT ABOUT A PERSON BY THE WAY HE/SHE HANDLES THESE THREE THINGS: A RAINY DAY, LOST LUGGAGE, AND TANGLED CHRISTMAS TREE LIGHTS.

—Maya Angelou

CHAPTER NINE

Let Go: Ignore All the Critics

Ignore everybody. —**Hugh McLeod**

One of the biggest blocks to creativity is this one: What will other people say about what I create? Will they love it? Will it be as good as the last one I did? Will it get good reviews? Will it get *any* reviews? Will someone buy it, publish it, review it, recommend it, collect it?

At a reading in Asheville recently, Barbara Kingsolver was asked about how she deals with bad reviews.

"I don't read them," she said. "I don't read *any* reviews anymore, good or bad. Because I realized that when I was reading reviews, I would tend to memorize the negative ones and ignore the positive ones."

Exactly. That's exactly it.

I can give a speech to 4,000 people and get lots of e-mail messages from people who were there and loved it. And I feel great about it until I get the first negative comment. Like Kingsolver, that's the one I focus on.

Ignore what other people say.
Create what you must,
not what people will buy.
Know your own strengths.
Build a creative tribe.

When I stay in the present the inner critic disappears. —**Susan Geddes**

The Tao Te Ching tells us this: "Care about people's approval and you will be their prisoner." There is no faster way to take yourself out of a creative space than by anxiously checking your Amazon page ranks every three minutes on the day your book is published. Trust me, I know.

Wondering if people will like your second book as much as the first will also thrust you right out of creativity and right into insanity and paralysis. Trust me, I know.

The only real way to be creative is to create. Without attachment to outcome. Without attachment to sales figures or blog hits. Without caring about the ways in which your work is dissected, criticized, or loved. But with a keen, overwhelming, burning, passionate focus on what it is you long to say more than anything else in the world. That's the thing. That's the only thing.

THEY CALL ME THE PAINTER OF DANCERS. THEY DON'T UNDERSTAND THAT THE DANCER HAS BEEN FOR ME A PRETEXT FOR PAINTING PRETTY FABRICS AND FOR RENDERING MOVEMENT.

—Edgar Degas

Do not be an art critic, but paint, therein lies salvation. —Paul Cézanne

Write like an orphan

If there are any of you at the back who do not hear me, please don't raise your hands because I am also nearsighted. —**W. H. Auden**

On Christmas Eve 2006 we gathered in front of the tree for our annual photograph—me and my tribe, my brother and his family, and my mom, a dozen of Scotch-Irish and three of Polish stock. My husband, John, and I were standing near the door to my mother's living room, adjusting the camera to make sure everyone was in the viewfinder, when I realized my mother wasn't there.

"MAMA," I yelled. "MAAAA-MA! Time for the picture—come on!" No answer. "WHERE *ARE* YOU?"

Just then she appeared at the door in her holiday sweater, slightly winded, her eyes bulging out a tad, holding out in front of her a small wallet-size photograph. I could see it was an old photo of her from the year she left the bank, wearing that blue dress Daddy bought her when she got promoted to banking officer, her hair wavy around her face, and wearing big bug-eyed plastic eyeglasses, like a welder's mask with bifocals.

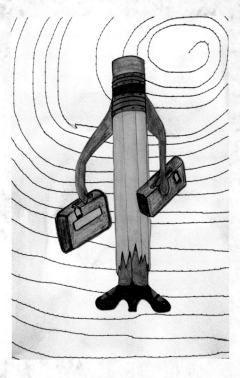

"Here," she said, her eyes popping out, her jaw clenched. "Here's the picture I want you to use with my obituary!"

Well, then, Merry Christmas and a Happy damn New Year, I thought to myself.

But before I could ask why finding this twenty-year-old photograph for her obituary had become so urgent on Christmas Eve, she said, "And I'll be writing *my own* obituary, thank you very much missy, because I've been reading your blog!"

With that, she turned on her heel in a way I had never seen, and took her place in the center of the idyllic dysfunctional family scene, looking for all the world just like her own obituary photograph I stood slack-jawed holding, if a few decades older.

My face went hot and red. John and I looked wildly at each other. "What?" I muttered to him, turning my back to the expectant scene like I was busy changing the location of the tripod. "She's reading my blog, John!" I hissed.

I had started writing my blog, 37days, two years earlier. It had never occurred to me that my own mother would find it, much less be reading it. *WHO TAUGHT THIS WOMAN HOW TO GOOGLE?* I yelled inside my head.

What kinds of revealing essays had she read about me? Exactly how long had she been reading it? Had she read the one about . . . ? Had I written something awful about her?

OH MY GOD, I have to race up the mountain to home and delete posts, I thought to myself as I smiled for the photograph, proof that we gathered on that evening in December. We left without Brownstone Front Cake or the traditional holiday hot tea made with Tang powdered drink mix like the astronauts drink so I could get home and stick my finger in the dike.

For weeks I thought she was angry and couldn't bring myself to post anything on the blog. This revelation stopped me cold. It's one thing for a complete stranger in Des Moines to know my innermost secrets; it's another altogether to have my *mother* reading along, her welding mask reflecting the glare of the computer screen as it tips upward to allow for bifocal reading.

When I finally asked if she was angry about the blog, she surprised me: "Oh, no, honey, I'm so proud of you!"

I now know that either answer was a death knell, in some respects. Either one. Whether she hated or liked it, my writing changed. **I was aware of an audience that had a face, and a history, and a heart. It changed what I was creating.**

My friend David Robinson is a talented painter and theater director, able to see into the spine of a story like no one else I know. David directed a one-man play in New York recently, having been called on by a superb young actor named Chris Domig to help him develop a compelling vision of the work. They worked together for weeks; when the play opened at the New York Fringe Festival, critics and audiences went crazy for it. In the review David sent, Chris was called "a startling young actor whose name will not remain unknown for long. Watching Domig . . . brings to mind a young Dustin Hoffman or Al Pacino when they were just starting off Broadway." (The reviews David didn't send, but I found online, were just as appreciative of the director.)

But it was the under-story that most fascinated me, the ways in which David taught Chris to ignore both critics and fans (and Mama, I imagine). It is a story I heard from both Chris and David as they looked back on the process, and it was what Chris defined as his biggest learning.

In preparing for his first preview audience, David kept reminding Chris not to pay attention to the audience, but to focus on what he was there to do, *his* story, *his* process, *his* art. That the audience didn't matter; whether they gave energy back to Chris during the performance or not was of no consequence and had nothing to do with Chris's work. "Just do the work," David told Chris. "Just do the work." As David has told me many times, writers write, actors act, painters paint. In none of those equations is there room for "and pay attention to what the audience is doing and change your work to fit that expectation or need."

"It was a disaster," Chris said when I heard his version of the story. He wasn't getting what he expected from the audience, and started adjusting his performance to meet them, to cajole them into responding, rather than following the spine of his own story, his own art.

David furiously made director's notes. "It was like watching a train wreck," he said. He knew immediately Chris was lost in his need to have the audience respond. "He forgot lines, he had to start over . . . painful," David said. Chris knew he was doomed when he looked over and David had stopped making director's notes. It was that bad.

> DON'T PAY ANY ATTENTION TO THE CRITICS—DON'T EVEN IGNORE THEM.
>
> —Samuel Goldwyn

And it was also his biggest learning. Only afterward did Chris garner all those glowing reviews—because he stayed in his process, in his art, and let the audience stay in theirs.

It is easy to fall prey to the question of whether other people like your art, your creative spirit. It is hard to ignore the chatter, the reviews, the family members, the people who walk past and say, "My five-year-old could do that" (which, by the way, should be taken as the very highest form of praise). We are creatures acclimated to seeking approval, to getting feedback, to satisfying our "audience," whether that is on Broadway, at our town's art show, or at our family's holiday celebrations.

> THEY NEVER RAISED A STATUE
> TO A CRITIC.
>
> —Martha Graham

This isn't true only of people who put their art into the world in the theater or art galleries—but of all of us. When a friend ridicules the handmade card you made, or your partner laughs at the idea of your taking painting classes, or a teacher slaps your hand for taking creative license with an assignment, it's the same as Chris Domig appearing in a New York play.

Painters paint, writers writer, actors act. They don't obsessively check their Amazon rankings or become paralyzed by those who give them negative reviews. By the time their art appears in the world, they are moving on to the next thing they feel compelled to say, that next painting to illustrate how they see the world, for no one else but them.

Writer Annie Dillard's writing "shed" was featured in Oprah's *O* magazine a few years ago. A gorgeous, simple building with nothing in it but a couch for napping and a large table with a laptop on it. When asked about her creative space, Dillard replied that there were no pictures of her family and friends in the building because when she writes, she needs to be an orphan. I know what she means; my Christmas Eve epiphany showed how easy it is to change our art to please, to avoid censure, to escape the questioning. Our challenge is to be a wildly curious orphan, disconnected from those who read or view our art, our creative expression.

give yourself 10

Word: Your goal is to express a part of yourself that stays hidden because you worry about what your friends or partner or mother would say. Write (or make art for ten minutes) your answer to this question: "What is my hidden secret?" The most human expression of ours—the one that includes our fears and secrets—is often the most potent source of the creative spirit, but we keep it hidden for fear of what others will think.

Image: Draw or create a collage that represents your audience—whether that is a literal audience if you are a performer, or the audience in your daily life (family, friends). Write the phrase "Write like an orphan" somewhere on this side.

give yourself 37

Using the question above, "What is my hidden secret?" as your prompt, either create a small index card artwork each day for 37 days, or write for five minutes a day on this question (or both!). To take this farther, if you're ready, leave your artwork or writing in public spaces for others to find—perhaps tucked into a library book—without staying to watch who finds it and their reaction. Or send it to PostSecret.com, a worldwide movement to gather "secrets" of people on post-cards. Move on, make the next artwork, write the next words.

A man who wants to lead the orchestra must turn his back on the crowd.
—Max Lucado

Embrace your clearness committee

Whenever I climb, I am followed by a dog named Ego. —**Friedrich Nietzche**

I came across a story this week that intrigued me. I could see myself in it, if truth be told, and perhaps if you squint, you can see some tiny part of yourself in it as well.

It's a story about Parker Palmer, a Quaker educator and author of the book *Let Your Life Speak,* in which he writes about a time he was offered the presidency of a large educational institution. He was thrilled with the thought of the status, pay raise, and influence he would have with the new position.

But before he accepted, he convened a group of friends to serve as what the Quakers have called since the 1600s a "Clearness Committee." The Clearness Committee protects individual identity and integrity while drawing on the wisdom of other people, allowing a person who is seeking clarity of vision on an issue to gain the wisdom of a group. **The sole mission of the Clearness Committee is not to have the right answers, but to craft respectful and supportive questions** that help the person find their own heart-centered answers. The Clearness Committee honors these inner answers—the ones that we must truly own.

At first the questions of the group centered on things like his vision for the institution. Then someone asked what seemed like a very simple question: "Parker, what would you like about being president?"

He started listing things he wouldn't like—the politics, raising money, no time for teaching. His friends asked again: "But what would you like?" Irritated, he answered, "I wouldn't like to give up my summer vacations, I wouldn't like . . ." For the third time they said, "But Parker, what would you like about it?"

Finally reaching deep inside, in a small voice, he called up the only honest answer he had, appalling himself as he uttered the words, "I guess what I'd really like most is getting my picture in the paper with the word *president* under it."

The group was silent. At last someone spoke: "Parker," he said, "can you think of an easier way to get your picture in the paper?" They all laughed and they all knew what his decision would be.

Certainly there's a message in his story about understanding and owning our personal motives, facing (and naming) the ego truth in what we do. Have you ever daydreamed about what your business card would look like with a more impressive-sounding title on it? ("Queen of All She Surveys" and "High Priestess of Perpetual Motion" are viable options.) Am I doing what I do because I really believe it needs doing—and (just think of the implications!) because I actually enjoy it? Or am I doing it just because it's a stepping-stone? Do I find myself doodling in the margins of books what my new title will be and what they'll say about me in the *New York Times*?

> [Attach yourself to those who advise you rather than praise you.
> —**Nicolas Boileau**]

When Emma was twelve, she was nominated to be in the Junior Honor Society. I found the announcement on the dining room table. When I gushed about the honor, she said, very quietly and without moving her head, that she wasn't going to join. "Why?" I gasped in a horrified you're-being-recognized-you-have-to-accept-it mother voice. She was uninterested. "My life is really full," she explained, "with things I actually like doing, like the softball team and playing tuba in the band." "But," I sputtered, "it'll look good on your college application." (Did I mention she was just twelve at the time?) And so, a lifetime of impressing others could have begun. Instead, she didn't join the honor society, choosing to run the bases rather than sit in meetings. She's my best teacher.

There's also another important message, I think, below the surface: Do I have a Clearness Committee, a circle of trust that I can convene at these important moments in my life? The answer for me is yes, though far flung—from Wellington to Hod HaSharon to California to DC to Decatur to Stellenbosch to Seattle and many places in between. Some of the best questions I've ever gotten are from half a world away. Perhaps I don't tap into their wisdom often enough. Or thank them enough. Or listen closely enough to the truth that emerges in response to their questions.

In another of his books, *A Hidden Wholeness,* Parker Palmer offers this view of a "circle of trust," akin to the Clearness Committee:

> BEWARE THAT YOU DO NOT LOSE THE SUBSTANCE BY GRASPING AT THE SHADOW.
>
> —Aesop

Here is one way to understand the relationships in a circle of trust: they combine unconditional love, or regard, with hopeful expectancy, creating a space that both safeguards and encourages the inner journey. In such a space, we are freed to hear our own truth, touch what brings us joy, become self-critical about our faults, and take risky steps toward change—knowing that we will be accepted no matter what the outcome.

I love that definition—**unconditional love with hopeful expectancy.** Who is in your circle of trust, both safeguarding and encouraging your inner journey, simultaneously nurturing and challenging you? With whom do you know you will be accepted no matter what the outcome?

Your creative challenge

Quick! Write down the names of the people on your Clearness Committee or in your circle of trust. Find a unique way to thank them for serving—and start using them. Also, get honest about the reasons you do what you do . . . perhaps there is a better way to get your picture in the paper.

give yourself 10

Word: Take this short quiz from a book by Marc Gafni, *Soul Prints,* which gets to some of the message for me: Name the five wealthiest people in the world. Name the last five winners of the Miss America contest. Name the last five people who have won the Nobel or Pulitzer Prize. Name the last half dozen Academy Award winners for best actor and actress. Name the last decade's worth of World Series winners. How did you do?

I know I did horrendously. The point is this: We forget yesterday's headliners. These people are the best in their fields. But the applause dies. Trophies tarnish. Achievements are forgotten. Accolades and awards are buried with their owners.

Here's another quiz. See how you do on this one. List a few teachers who aided your journey through school. Name three friends who have helped you through a difficult time. Name five people who have taught you something worthwhile. Think of a few people who have made you feel appreciated and special. Name half a dozen heroes whose stories have inspired you.

I think you get the point. I know I did. Write these people down. Embrace your Clearness Committee.

Image: Create an image of your Clearness Committee—not the people in it, necessarily, but how you will feel in it.

give yourself 37

Identify five people you would invite to serve on your Clearness Committee, keeping in mind that choosing at least a few people whose worldviews are different from your own will be important. What challenge are you facing now that you would ask for their help with? Now invite them, and find a way to convene your Clearness Committee.

Build your own Fallingwater

At age 20, we worry about what others think of us. At 40, we don't care what they think of us. At 60, we discover they haven't been thinking about us at all. —**Jock Falkson**

I once designed a three-day conference on diversity for a professional organization whose members are school food service personnel—by their own

definition, they are the cafeteria ladies who serve food in schools across the nation.

The conference was an opportunity for them to raise questions and concerns about the increasing diversity they were facing, both within their workforce and in the schools they serve. It was a rich, full weekend of honest dialogue. And one of the issues they raised was one I hear often among English speakers about their increasingly diverse workplaces: "When our workers speak Spanish or Hmong, I feel like they're talking about me and I don't like it. I want it to stop. I think they should have to speak only English at work."

After hearing them voice their discomfort, I responded gently: Is it within the realm of human possibility that you are not the center of their universe and that they, in fact, might have something better (more interesting, more relevant, more fun) than you to talk about? After all, as Falkson says, "at 60, we discover they haven't been thinking about us at all." Perhaps we'd be better served if we realized that before we reached sixty?

That's a prelude to the real story. Ultimately, in the end, it is a story about the waterfall over which Frank Lloyd Wright's Fallingwater house is built in Mill Run, Pennsylvania. But it gets there by way of a high school reunion.

This past weekend I got a fantastic surprise, an e-mail from an old high school friend, one of my favorite people then—we had spent those years hanging out together, running, playing in the marching band together. My Lord, man, we even survived Elvis's death and disco together!

We cut quite a rug on the lighted dance floor, like upright, slightly frenetic synchronized swimmers gyrating and flinging each other around to the tunes of the Bee Gees and Donna Summer—a dance done for the benefit of others, ultimately. If I'm ever nominated to the Supreme Court, I'll deny all knowledge of ABBA.

I hadn't heard from Steve for many, many years—decades, even—so many years that we had to start over, not remembering what we knew about each other's lives since those happy days of adolescence and—to be honest—not sure what we even remembered from those days, either.

Our reconnect was all going so swimmingly well until he asked a simple question: "If there's a thirtieth reunion next year, will you go?"

Huh?

Excuse me, the young inside Me thought, *you must have the wrong person. You must be mistaken. I can't possibly have graduated from high school thirty years ago; you're thinking of my mother.*

After going quickly through the requisite stages—denial (*I'm not old enough!*), anger (*I'm too old!*), bargaining (*please let me lose weight and get my eyebrows done first*), depression (*I'm old!*), and acceptance (*I'm old, which means I'm still alive, hallelujah!*)—I recovered from the shock long enough to put Steve on hold and get a personal trainer on the other line to set up intensive daily sessions since I only had eighteen months to get into the best shape of my life, to regain that athletic, thin, blue-jeaned body of thirty years ago so I can act nonchalantly like I've looked like that all along. Only eighteen months to get rich and build the dream house and buy that red Ferrari and whatever else

To write is to locate my own address inside my head. —E. M. Forster

people do besides eat themselves into a coma with Ding Dongs when they're trying to impress people whose names they can't remember and who have not figured into their lives in even the smallest of ways in the past thirty years.

Another high school friend and I were e-mailing afterward about the reunion—"I'll go if you go"—and we both had trouble remembering the names of many of our classmates. **So if I don't remember their names, why be so intent on impressing them? I wonder.** Is it possible that they don't remember my name, either, and that they don't much care if I'm a size 8, or if I have gray hair, or if my eyebrows are reacting to gravity and eating my eyelids?

> [**Paper suffers everything and blushes at nothing.**
> —**Proverb**]

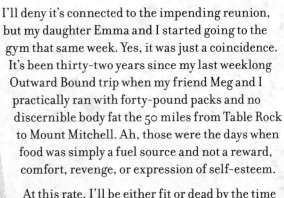

I'll deny it's connected to the impending reunion, but my daughter Emma and I started going to the gym that same week. Yes, it was just a coincidence. It's been thirty-two years since my last weeklong Outward Bound trip when my friend Meg and I practically ran with forty-pound packs and no discernible body fat the 50 miles from Table Rock to Mount Mitchell. Ah, those were the days when food was simply a fuel source and not a reward, comfort, revenge, or expression of self-esteem.

At this rate, I'll be either fit or dead by the time that reunion rolls around.

And, finally, to Fallingwater.

Fallingwater is recognized as one of Frank Lloyd Wright's best works. In a 1991 poll of members of the American Institute of Architects, it was voted "the best all-time work of American architecture." It is considered a supreme example of his concept of organic architecture, which promotes harmony between man and nature through design so well integrated with its site that buildings, furnishings, and surroundings become part of a unified, interrelated composition. That's what the guidebooks say.

When I look at this house, I admire his desire that the inhabitants become part of nature, not separate observers of it. I get that. And I think there is much about it that is beautiful, I do. But when I see that overhang of concrete, I'm always first struck by the fact that while you can hear it, the very water that the house is named for is unseeable from the house itself.

The house was designed in 1935 for E. J. Kaufman who, when presented with the plans, said, "I thought you would place the house near the waterfall, not over it." Mr. Wright said quietly, "E. J., I want you to live with the waterfall, not just to look at it, but for it to become an integral part of your lives."

He did build the house around a favorite rock of Mr. Kaufman's, one on which he loved to sun himself. That rock forms the big stone fireplace inside. And from the Great Room a set of stairs enables you to walk down and stand on a tiny platform in the middle of the stream.

I don't doubt the genius of this house, dubbed "the building of the century," and I'll admit to more than a modicum of ignorance about Wright's work, but here's my take on it: He didn't build the structure for the person living in the house, but for the observer and maybe, even, for himself.

You can't see the waterfall from the house. Standing where we are, looking at the house with the water below, we can see what drew Kaufman to this spot in the first place. Sitting in his built-in cantilevered concrete orange-cushioned dining nook, he could do no more than hear it. The occupant, the person living there, is secondary to Wright's vision, ultimately.

LET THE IMPORTANT THING BE HOW YOU LOOK AT THINGS AND NOT WHAT YOU ARE LOOKING AT.

—André Gide

I wonder how many times I have done that, building a life that is revered from the outside but that is overshadowing and hiding my waterfall, the source of all my energy, from me. Who am I building my life for? For the person living in the house, or for the observer—for me or for those high school classmates, for the waterfall or for the architect?

Take yourself out of the center of other people's universe—it will free you up and will let the universe turn more easily. And in a metaphoric and literal sense, let others speak whatever language makes them feel whole and human. It doesn't detract from your wholeness and your humanity, but adds to it. Build your own Fallingwater, your art, one where you can see the waterfall, where there are no concrete overhangs shadowing the very source of who you are, the "there" that attracted you to yourself in the first place, that water falling. Build your house for you, not for observers who, by the way, aren't looking anyway.

give yourself 10

Word: What are some things people tell you you're good at? Do you like doing those things? What do you have a real yes for? Is there a gap between what *they* say and what your real yes is about?

Image: Trust your own perspective—ask yourself: What's the thing I most want to see? Where do I need to stand (metaphorically) in order to see it? Create an image of it.

give yourself 37

Notice each day how we obscure the things we love. I have many artifacts from my childhood—things that evoke powerful, deep memories for me . . . and many of them are stuffed into drawers and boxes. Do we have so much that we cannot see the waterfall? Just notice what we obscure—without judgment. And each day, spent ten minutes uncovering those things you love— whether that means cleaning out the boxes in your attic a little bit at a time or painting your dining room that deep yellow you've always wanted.

The least touchable object in the world is the eye.
—Rudolf Arnheim

Circle the ring again

You're not obligated to win. You're obligated to keep trying to do the best you can every day. —**Marian Wright Edelman**

She looked so small up on that horse.

Big black helmet, her dark brown curly hair captured in an industrial-strength hairnet, her jodhpurs tucked into tall black boots. She was nervous, I could tell. Her first show in a very long time, and this one seemed huge—a real show, not a schooling show.

Three big rings, hundreds of people and horses; it was a new thing for her, this sudden dip into a bigger pool. **My heart ached and soared for her, and yet I knew she needed space,** not close contact. And so I stood back, just at the edge of her peripheral vision, in case she needed to touch someone for grounding.

Matthew, her horse, was new to her, too. This would be the first time they had ridden together in a show. She's a hunter/jumper, riding English. I tried one lesson, because she asked me to. THERE IS NOTHING TO HOLD ON TO ON AN ENGLISH SADDLE. WHERE IS THE HORN? THIS HORSE IS THIRTY FEET TALL! My future as an Olympic Equestrian Athlete died right there with that realization. I stayed for an hour. I call that a Gold Medal performance.

Not so, Emma. She is born to be around horses. And yet, I watched her sixteen-year-old self mount Matty for her turn in the ring with such an out-pouring of desire to save her. She was twitchy nervous, and he knew it.

They entered the ring. I don't know anything about riding; I just know she is the best rider who ever got on a horse, with the straightest posture and the cleanest boots. John shines them to military sheen.

There was a certain pattern to the jumps that each young rider had to memorize in order to get full points for the ride. Emma had watched the first few riders, and I could see her steady gaze jump through the plan in her head as she entered.

Looking good. My heart in my throat, that mother part of me that always wants me to save her, the part that has to be quieted in order for her to learn, grow, be herself and not just an extension of myself.

Matthew started trotting as she asked. They approached the first jump, all eyes on her. This a child who used to cry when she had to give a book report at school, who used to ask me to write out a script for her to use when she called a friend on the phone: "Hi, Mrs. _____, this is Emma Ptak. I'm a classmate of your daughter, _____. Is she available to talk?" And then, of course, a script for when the mother said yes and another one for if she said no. And good Lord, never mind if someone other than the mother answered the phone. The possibilities were endless, just like life. **Before long, of course, she didn't need the scripts anymore.**

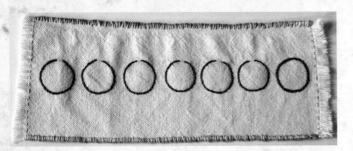

And so here she was, the center of all attention. The other girls on horses watched their competition, other parents watched a girl who couldn't possibly be as talented, smart, beautiful as their daughters, and I watched my heart ride straight by me on a horse.

Matthew trotted. They approached the first jump and he simply stopped. "A refusal!" I heard someone say near me. *"He refused!"*

There was a time when Emma would have simply trotted that horse back out of the ring and gone home, never to return, so mortified would she have been. Imagine my surprise when she sat still for a moment, then regrouped, turned Matthew to one side, and trotted in a big circle right back up to that jump.

He refused again.

Now, I thought to myself. *Now she will run away in tears.*

Imagine my surprise when she turned him to the left again, trotting in a wide circle to approach again.

He refused.

Six times my little Emma turned Matthew to the left and tried again. The crowd was quiet, watching. I was in tears at what I knew—and they didn't know—about what it took for her to do that.

On the seventh try, Matthew jumped.

He jumped.

Circle the ring again.

Your creative challenge

Continue not for the show ribbon, but to do the thing itself, to show yourself (not others) that you can.

give yourself 10

Word: "Don't think of it as a failure. Think of it as a time-released success."

—Robert Orben

What is the "jump" your horse keeps refusing? How does it feel in that ring?

Image: Create a collage of words associated with how it feels for you at that jump when the horse refuses. Do you want to run screaming from the ring?

give yourself 37

Every day for 37 days, start your day with the task you most fear, dread, or that is the most difficult for some reason—the thing you keep putting off. Clear your desk (or mind) and work only on that task for thirty minutes each morning. Don't multitask, but work solely on getting over that "jump." Just for thirty minutes each morning (or each day if the mornings don't work for you). Make note each evening of any discoveries you make about the ways in which attention changes your relationship with the obstacle.

A CHAMPION IS SOMEONE WHO GETS UP, EVEN WHEN HE CAN'T.

—Jack Dempsey

Don't export your peaches

The flat sound of my wooden clogs on the cobblestones, deep, hollow and powerful, is the note I seek in my painting. —**Paul Gauguin**

I had two brushes with greatness last week.

The first arrived in the mail. I was shocked to open a 9x12-inch envelope and find a handwritten missive to me from none other than Billy Collins, a poet whose use of the English language I greatly admire.

Imagine! A real honest-to-goodness letter from Billy Collins written on the front cover of the Dodge Poetry Festival! And I quote:

My dearest Patti, you veritable single golden sugar cube in my skinny latte, my painted pony walking across the Atlantic, my bread and my knife, my crystal goblet and—somehow—my wine . . . Imagine my surprise, dear Patti, when I was walking along a tiny path composing a poem about nature in my tiny noggin—perhaps something about one enormous sky and about a million empty branches—when all of a sudden, a man appeared from nowhere, lunging at me and thrusting this Festival program under my nose, asking for an autograph for some woman named Patti who adores me. And then it hit me—of course! That Patti! I read 37days every week; you are my muse, my inspiration, my everything! We really must get together and read poetry together in the desert, or go on a picnic and avoid the lightning. With my undying love and gratitude for your mentioning me incessantly on 37days, Yours —Billy

Well, I guess it was actually a Dodge Poetry Festival program with his name scrawled on the bottom right of the front cover, but I know how to read between the lines.

That's all to say this: A 37days reader, Steve Sherlock, when coming face-to-face with Billy Collins on a dirt path at the Dodge Poetry Festival, had the presence of mind to ask Mr. Collins for an autograph so he could send it to me! What a wonderful gift! It is sitting prettily in my office beside the autographed photo of, well, someone else.

The second brush with greatness came last Thursday when I had lunch with one of my great artistic heroes, a multimedia artist and musician, the brilliant Laurie Anderson. Imagine!

That's to say that I spent my lunch hour in an audience listening to her speak. But there were only fifty of us there, so I was in great proximity and I did get close enough to her afterward to hand her my card with a tiny note on the back explaining her impact both on me, and now, on Emma. I'm sure she'll be in touch soon. Having been that close, I feel completely justified to pepper my conversation with phrases such as this: "What a coincidence! Laurie Anderson said that to me just the other day!"

With dimples to dive into, Laurie Anderson has long influenced the music world, and the world of multimedia performance. It started for me in 1980 with "O Superman," from her album *Big Science,* then *Mister Heartbreak,* then her work with the über-brilliant (and, ahem, hot) Philip Glass, and who could forget her *Songs and Stories from Moby Dick*? Certainly not this American literature major.

There are only a handful of musicians I would pay to see in concert. Okay, there are exactly ten: Philip Glass, Tracy Chapman, Joan Armatrading, Johnny Cash (before, well, you know), Doc Watson, k. d. lang, Lyle Lovett, Tom Waits, the Kronos Quartet, and Laurie Anderson. Okay, eleven including Bonnie Raitt. Am I missing anyone? Okay, the Jethro Tull gang back in the day, along with the Talking Heads. I'd put Laurie Anderson at the very top of that list. I first saw her perform live in an intimate little theater in Washington, DC, in 2002.

Yet when The Laurie Anderson came back to my little tiny burg recently, I was not here. I was on a plane flying home from Somewhere Not Here. Sob. Sob more. Rant. Rave. Lament loudly. Whine even. There was nothing to do but send the fabulous Emma in my place.

I think it might have changed her life. I was meant to miss that show so she could go.

Laurie was playing *The End of the Moon,* a piece that emerged from her year as an artist in residence at the National Aeronautics and Space Administration (NASA). "How was it?" I asked breathlessly from the airport, cursing my fate at awaiting a delayed Delta flight while Emma basked in the glory that is Laurie Anderson without me.

"Awesome. It was just awesome." Emma is not one for hyperbole, or bole of any kind for that matter, so I was struck by the enormity of her response. "The first notes she played on her electric violin made my seat shake and went into my bones," she continued excitedly. "It was just awesome!" she fairly well shrieked.

She seemed transformed by the experience, by her proximity to Art, her experience of what one reviewer called Anderson's NASA-fueled vision of inner and outer space.

The focus of the night's performance—space—was especially wonderful for this teenager who long dreamed of being an astronomer.

I needed more details . "I don't really know how to describe it," she said when I pressed for more information. "It made me think more about what could be turned into song, a poem, a piece of literature."

Like opening the whole world to art.

As *Rolling Stone* wrote, "Laurie Anderson is a singer-songwriter of crushing poignancy—a minimalist painter of melancholy moods who addresses universal themes in the vernacular of the commonplace." I think that is exactly what Emma was saying, in fewer words. Our whole lives are art, Emma realized, and ours—not just poets and musicians Up There On Stage—but every wee human, even us. Even a fourteen-year-old like she was at the time.

Shortly after having lunch with my new pal Laurie, a friend told me—apropos of nothing, it seemed at the time—that the best peaches aren't found in Georgia. They're grown there, but the best ones are exported to markets outside Georgia. A colleague from Florida confirmed the same thing about selected Florida produce. The best beer isn't found where it is brewed; nor is the best caviar enjoyed at its place of origin. I found that fascinating. Isn't that what we do when we act better for company than for our own families, when we spend more time pleasing strangers than pleasing ourselves, when we adore celebrities and not our own Selves?

I started by saying that I had two brushes with greatness this week, but that's not true—it was far more than that. It included all those people I met in Iowa this week, and the man named Dennis on the plane from Des Moines to Atlanta who accounts for one of the Absolute Best Conversations I've Ever Had, and the kids at tonight's Halloween party at the local recreation center (Tess won the best costume award!), and my family, *and all of you.* All those wooden clogs on all those cobblestones. The deep, hollow, powerful sounds of everyday life becoming art.

Your creative challenge

My recent encounters with Billy and Laurie remind me of the time I had dinner with Garrison Keillor in Minneapolis. And not just in the same country, state, county, and town, but in the very same restaurant and in very nearly the same room.

Yet as much as I revere Billy Collins and Laurie Anderson and as much as I turn to look when Garrison Keillor walks in the room, **perhaps it is the sound of my own clogs on the cobblestones that is my one true art.** I shouldn't abdicate that art to Artists; it is my own.

That's not to say we can't dream of having a lightning picnic with Billy Collins, a pirate romp with Johnny Depp, or an electric duet with Laurie Anderson, but there are also humans all around us who deserve our awe, our silent and full and best reverence. Including our own precious selves.

And don't export your best peaches. Keep them for those close to home.

give yourself 10

Word: "What greater gift than being able to communicate and enable our fellow humans the sensations of being alive." —Nicoletta Baumeister

What are the first words that come to mind when I ask you to describe the sensations of being alive?

Image: What images denote ordinary "aliveness" to you?

give yourself 37

More than likely, the images that you created above are ordinary things, not Great Things. Everyday things that together create what we know as "aliveness." For 37 days, make a note (one per index card) of what represented "aliveness" that day for you. What sensations told you that you were alive?

PART THREE
Art Yearning

Life is your art.

An open, aware heart is your camera.

A oneness with your world is your film.

Your bright eyes, your easy smile

is your museum.

—*Ansel Adams*

home

have you ever hoarded
your dreams? fearful that
if you shared them someone
might steal them? even worse
we sometimes fear we're
not worthy of our own dreams
so we quitclaim them
to others saying here take
my magic i won't be
needing it and i'll even
throw in the wand

we fill our days writing to
do lists and thinking up goals
but dreams don't like to be
analyzed they're not comfortable
on the couch they prefer to
take up residence in the heart
where they can use ancient keys
to unlock doors spilling
liquid light of recognition into
our sighs of relief when we
realize we're home

—*Marilyn Maciel*

CHAPTER TEN
Create Life As If

We are the yearning creatures of this planet. —**Robert Olen Butler**

Life is yearning meeting obstacle.

Perhaps, as *The Last Lecture*'s Randy Pausch told us, "Brick walls are there for a reason. They let us prove how badly we want things." Brick walls are, in fact, the stuff of life. Dealing with them makes the story move forward, just as Little Red Riding Hood depends on the Big Bad Wolf to be a story. And all stories—yours and mine included—depend on yearning. We desire something, someone—and something stands in the way. More often than not, it's the journey that stands in the way—we have to make a trek and most of us just want to do an "I dream of Jeannie" and be there without traveling through space and time to get there.

Open up.
See more.
Live deeper.
Let yourself yearn.

"We yearn," says writer Robert Olen Butler. "We are the yearning creatures of this planet. There are superficial yearnings, and there are truly deep ones always pulsing beneath, but every second we yearn for *something*."

I think we yearn to create. More than anything, I think we yearn to create. And **creating comes in many forms, though we've narrowed our definition of it to art forms.** Parenting is creating. Teaching is creating. Working is creating. Being a friend is creating. It all is.

Life itself is yearning. That is the story of life—yearning hitting up against obstacles. So often we play the victim, blaming others (other people, other circumstances, other choices) for the obstacles. What if the obstacles *are* the point, the measure against which we can find the depth of the yearning itself? Learning about fiction is learning about life, isn't it? Fiction, Butler says, is the art form of human yearning. But yearning is often missing from what we are reading (and possibly from what we are living?):

"You may admire, maybe you have a kind of 'smart' reaction—but nothing resonates in the marrow of your bones, and the reason is that the character's yearning is not manifest."

"The difference between the desires expressed in entertainment fiction and literary fiction is only a difference of level," Butler says. "Instead of: *I want a man, a woman, wealth, power, or to solve a mystery or to drive a stake through a vampire's heart,* a literary desire is on the order of: *I yearn for self, I yearn for an identity, I yearn for a place in the universe, I yearn to connect to the other.*" At what level am I yearning? You? Am I living an entertainment fiction or a literary fiction?

"Fiction is about human beings and human emotions," Butler said in a recent interview. "Fiction is not about ideas. Students are writing from their heads, and that's the problem. Art does not come from the mind; it does not come from ideas. It comes from the place where you dream. Because they are writing from their heads, they are abstracting and generalizing, and interpreting and analyzing people's feelings, characters' feelings. They aren't expressing feeling. They lose track of yearning." Is this also true not only of students writing, but of people living?

Desire is what drives plot, the stories that make up our lives. At what level are we yearning? On the level of *I want an iPhone or a Lexus,* or on the level of *I want to speak my truth; I want to live my truth; I want to find out who I am, not who you think I am; I want to create?*

The problem is, I've found, that the yearning is often for ideal conditions, a yearning that only keeps us out of our creative selves. Stop yearning for ideal conditions: the right space, the right skills, the right ideas and mentor and conditions. Wittgenstein wrote his *Tractatus* while a soldier. Einstein worked in a patent office with one window and a playground right outside, then went home to do his brilliant thinking at a dining room table. Harry Potter started on napkins in a café. Beautiful, haunting pieces of music were composed by prisoners in concentration camps in Germany.

LIFE IS A GREAT BIG CANVAS, AND YOU SHOULD THROW ALL THE PAINT YOU CAN ON IT.

—Danny Kaye

The right conditions won't help.

In a writing class here in Asheville, North Carolina, a colleague in the workshop I attended had written a story about a writer with writer's block. The instructor, novelist Tommy Hays, kept asking about the writer's desk when we, as a group, were workshopping the writer's story. Finally, exasperated by Tommy's insistence on asking questions about the character's desk, one of the group said, "Tommy. What is up with your fascination with this character's desk?"

In his inimitable southern drawl, Tommy answered: "We-ll, the character's a writer, but we don't even see his desk. I have to at least see him try."

The dynamic behind our life's story is plot, which Butler defines (brilliantly, I believe) as "the attempt to fulfill the yearning and the world's attempt to thwart that.

"When you write a story you need to make sure that something is at stake. It doesn't need to be an external thing; it must have inner magnitude, though. Your character's yearning is deep and important; you need to treat it with respect."

Maybe **when we live our story we also need to make sure that something is at stake, something with inner magnitude.** And we have to at least see ourselves try.

What is my epiphany of yearning, where "the sensual details accumulate around a moment in which the deepest yearning of the main character shines forth"? Am I moving so quickly that I won't recognize that moment when it arrives, but only brush past it?

I want to sense my most fundamental yearnings by writing about them. Really writing about them. Not the writing you do at the surface, once in a while, when it's convenient, no. Not the kind that you do after the daily problems like taxes and mortgage payments are resolved, but the kind where you do it daily, to get to that unconscious place where lines connect as if by magic, and things unfold. That unfolding is something I must wait for, work for.

Yearn deeper to get to. I want to appreciate that the story—my life story—only moves forward because my yearnings meet obstacles, and to embrace the brick walls as integral to the story itself, acknowledging that the plot of my life is the meeting of deep yearning bumping up against obstacles, a world set on thwarting it. I want to rejoice in the sparks when those things collide. Own them, don't blame them. Allow myself to yearn.

"If we were a medical school, and you were here as a med student practicing appendectomies, you'd take your work very seriously because you would imagine that some night at two a.m. someone is going to waltz into your emergency room and you're going to have to save their life. Well, my friends, someday at eight p.m. someone is going to walk into your concert hall and bring you a mind that is confused, a heart that is overwhelmed, a soul that is weary. Whether they go out whole again will depend partly on how well you do your craft . . . Frankly, ladies and gentlemen, I expect you not only to master music; I expect you to save the planet. If there is a future wave of wellness on this planet, of harmony, of peace, of an end to war, of mutual understanding, of equality, of fairness, I don't expect it will come from a government, a military force or a corporation. I no longer even expect it to come from the religions of the world, which together seem to have brought us as much war as they have peace. If there is a future of peace for humankind, if there is to be an understanding of how these invisible, internal things should fit together, I expect it will come from the artists, because that's what we do. As in the concentration camp and the evening of 9/11, the artists are the ones who might be able to help us with our internal, invisible lives."

—excerpts from Karl Paulnack's speech to
incoming freshmen at the Boston Conservatory

Epilogue

UNCOVER YOUR OWN PENTIMENTO

> *Old paint on a canvas, as it ages, sometimes becomes transparent. When that happens it is possible, in some pictures, to see the original lines: a tree will show through a woman's dress, a child makes way for a dog, a large boat is no longer on an open sea. That is called* pentimento *because the painter "repented," changed his mind. Perhaps it would be as well to say that the old conception, replaced by a later choice, is a way of seeing and then seeing again.* —**from the Introduction to Lillian Hellman's *Pentimento***

There are layers to us, *scriptio inferior*, underwriting, shown clear like the Grand Canyon reveals its strata when laid bare, like a seven-layer dip or a tiramisu or, in some cases, like a mine that has caved in deep inside us. Send down a camera, are we still alive? Save us. Some of the layers emerge over time like a pentimento, as translucent. We become the aggregate of our pigment over many years—and some layers reveal themselves only with intense searching, like a palimpsest, the provenance of which may not be evident to the naked eye. Look, look.

Pentimento:

n.pl. pentimenti

> An underlying image in a painting, as an earlier painting, part of a painting or original draft that is revealed usually when the top layer of paint becomes transparent with age. From the Italian *pentimento*, correction; from *pentire*, to repent.

If we live as if on a painter's canvas, the movement of our feet or crutches or wheels in paint creates our portrait. Ours is a canvas bordered only by time and not some massive imposing frame; paint layers show through only over the passing of the ages, ours.

Only at the very end do our layers become fully apparent, the paint having become transparent. At old age, or at some age (I imagine the rapidity of transparency varies from person to person), we are finally laid bare, the trees showing through our dress, the child making way for a dog, as Lillian Hellman has written. **The "what might have been" is overpainted by "what was."**

I walked down a long hall in a nursing home today, and as I traversed those halls with Tess by my side, there were women—always women—sitting in doorways staring at me or not, or calling to Tess like some wheeled siren, smiling a smile of remembering or of envy or of delight, their skin transparent like onion vellum, so thin I could see the workings of their veins, those roadways to living.

I wondered what they might repent or regret, seeing life from that chair now; what original sketches were showing through in preparation for the bright blaze and conflagration that would mark the end—or the beginning? Old, translucent skin, like oils that have grown thin over time, letting the past emerge, those original intentions like veins, some big like aorta, some minuscule, each contributing its small part to the vital network that carries life.

Uncover your pentimento.
Love the layers of your self.
Leave your voice behind.

There, there, just in the doorway of Room 119, I can almost see what would have been, what almost was, what might have been if she had said yes instead of no to life. In Room 141, I can only yet see what was; the downturn of our mouths at that age tells much about how we have worn our faces through time. We cover and cover and cover regrets with thicker paint, until we can paint no more, our hands too arthritic to hold the brush; it all falls away.

As poet JL Williams has written:

> I realise I threw something away that was of importance to me. I want it back, I can remember the existence of it but the image has been painted

over. The thing itself is gone, the specificity of it, the texture of its construc-
tion, the markings which made it individual, the inscription of its name
upon its tongue. Because it was I who disposed of it, and I, singularly,
who possess this exact memory of its existence, I am responsible for find-
ing it or for creating it again out of the impression it made in me.

A pentimento, that under-image, shadow of an earlier painting, a part, a draft, a fragment that shows through, from the Latin *paenitere,* to repent.

Or let's say, instead of oils on fabric, our lives are made of earth, pressed down under immense heat and colored with the pressure of events done and not done: We are the Grand Canyon, deep oranges indicating heat, brilliant pink telling of decisions made or not made, perhaps.

Such a cross section was the image drawn by a most wonderful Belgian man one summer in a class I taught on storytelling. "Draw the map of your life," we said to the class, and were gifted with fantastic images—circles and paths and remarkable renderings, some literal, some not—and this one of his life's orange and green and pink and black strata from Bob Elgen. I was struck by the simple extravagant beauty of it, the way he had translated living into strata.

"What is that black dot?" I asked, completely enamored with his image, hardly able to contain my excitement at it, my clear and certain recognition of it. "That first black dot," he said quietly, "that is when my father died." **I recognized the rightness of it, knew it immediately, yes.** The lines created a whole, there was rightness in that green off to the edge,
truth in those sketchy lines, this
exposition of a life, that placement,
the metaphors implicit in those
colors, that leaped to meaning from
event.

Our Grand Canyons tell us what
has gone before—we can clearly see
history there as we stand dwarfed
by it, surrounded both by what has
gone before and by what is missing: Erosion has done its job. A rock
formation rising 1,800 feet above the
high-desert plain in San Juan County,

New Mexico, the famous "winged rock" called Shiprock gives us the opposite: There, we are in the middle of everything that is not left—by absence, we are to infer what was here before. And so too, with our lives, those internal canyons.

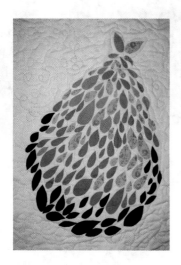

Or perhaps instead of paint or sand, we are brick, front-loaded on an old truck and placed, rectangle by rectangle, to build a majestic department store, the first of its kind, the kind with a sign painted on the side to display its glory, then only a shadow, then faded more, then overpainted, the traces of things left behind. I wonder what my signs say, those ones that have been painted over. Perhaps their reading emerges in my writing, now. Perhaps they will only be discovered hundreds of years hence, and look merely quaint, like ads for pinking shears and Dr. Tucker's pain pills.

Or perhaps we are like those plastinated bodies laid bare in Body Worlds, except instead of veins and organs, we are sliced to reveal heartaches and joys and regrets, each a different color, some pastel and some vivid blues and reds. Or like the overlays of plastic sheets in the old Encyclopedia Brittanica housed in the narrow hall of my childhood home—peeling up arteries to reveal the liver, layering skin on bones with a flick of the wrist.

Perhaps our life's composition originally had a head or a hand in a slightly different place, or a figure that was originally planned is no longer found in the final painting, dead or displaced or ignored or rebuked or misunderstood. What we do with that change in composition is what matters, not what we intended to do.

What we see as we stand behind that red velvet rope, peering into our life's retrospective—trying to find the narrative thread in the catalog ("How does this show fit together?" "My toddler could paint that," "What on earth is the title of that monstrosity?" "I love the interplay of teal and ocher")—is not what we intended to paint, but what, in fact, we painted.

Palimpsest. A palimpsest is also a "was," a manuscript page that has been written on, scraped off, and used again. With the passing of time, the faint

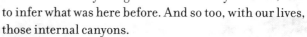

Vermeer found a life's work in the corner of a room. —Irwin Greenberg

remains of the former writing that had been washed from parchment or vellum, using milk and oat bran, reappear enough to allow scholars to discern the text, the *scriptio inferior*. One of the most famous, the Archimedes Palimpsest, is the work of the great Syracusan mathematician copied onto parchment in the tenth century and overwritten by a liturgical text in the twelfth century. Shadows emerge when looked for—sometimes, as in this case, they are more important than the primary text, the public one.

I imagine our lives as a text, written into the margins, the *o*'s of past writing forming *e*'s of today's verse, the old writing never disappearing, not fully.

And not just on paper or vellum, but skies: Ancient lunar craters whose relief has disappeared from subsequent volcanic outpourings, leaving only a "ghost" of a rim, are also known as palimpsests. In medicine the term is used to describe an episode of acute anterograde amnesia without loss of consciousness, brought on by the ingestion of alcohol or other substances: "alcoholic palimpsest." In forensic science, it describes objects placed over one another to establish the sequence of events at an accident or crime scene.

> SOMETIMES I JUST WANT TO BE PASSIONATE ABOUT SOMETHING. I DON'T EVEN KNOW IF IT'S PAINTING. BUT I HAVEN'T FOUND ANYTHING ELSE THAT COMES CLOSE.
>
> —Holly Monacelli

Architects imply palimpsest as a ghost—an image of what once was, those tarred rooflines that remain after a neighboring structure has been demolished, removed stairs that still show as an amputated arm still tingles, dust lines from a relocated refrigerator, all informing us of the built past. We each have a built past—what signs remain from it?

Our brains are human palimpsests, says Thomas De Quincey in his "Palimpsest of the Human Brain": *Everlasting layers of ideas, images, feelings, have fallen upon your brain softly as light. Each succession has seemed to bury all that went before. And yet, in reality, not one has been extinguished . . .*

In each case—pentimento and palimpsest—what is necessary for them to finally appear is the passage of moment after moment after moment, and the accumulated iterations that time brings with it. Read them, draw them, plumb them. They have served well as your canvas, shoring up today's painting.

Whether from absence or from erosion or massive volcanic upheaval or the simple rings of aging forests, our maps are both there and they are not there, not yet. Look, look. See and then see again. They will rise to the surface at some point—be ready to read them. And perhaps, after all this looking, **it is not what we have painted—or written—but that we have painted, that we have written.**

Considering the ways in which so many of us waste our time, what would be wrong with a world in which everybody were writing poems? While you are writing your poem, there's one less scoundrel in the world. I don't think there could ever be too many poets. By writing poetry, even those poems that fail and fail miserably, we honor and affirm life. We say,

"We loved the earth but could not stay."

—Ted Kooser, *Poetry Home Repair Manual: Practical Advice for Beginning Poets*

We loved the earth but could not stay. But here, here—here's the record of how much we loved it—all those paper dresses, monogrammed pancakes, wild celebrations of everyday life. If we embody a creativity spirit rather than learn it, make time for it, buy supplies for it, or take classes about it, perhaps our life *will* be a painting, a poem. Perhaps it already is.

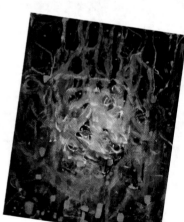

Be ordinary: *put down your clever*

See more: *turn around and look*

Get present: *show up like magic*

Catch fire: *please lick the art*

Clear ground: *stop trying so hard*

Let go: *ignore all the critics*

Stop trying to explain everything.
Stop trying to capture everything.

Just live it. Fling yourself in. Get lost more often. Make every single day a finger painting where getting messy is at least half the point.

Leave a part of yourself behind. The magic part. The hot, chaotic, unsure, beautiful part.

Write stuff down. Color over it with a crayon. Leave a box of those pages for the rest of us to find, know, hold on to long after you've gone, try to decipher in the context of our own lives, from our own ground.

That's the only way we will ever remember your voice.

Go Farther

You don't need to look for answers outside yourself. No, you truly don't. You've enough data and information and knowledge and wisdom in the stories of your own life to keep you busy for a long time, if you can but pay attention to them, be mindful of them.

But sometimes we all need a little inspiration. When that moment hits, here's the "short list" of my go-to books:

Art and Fear: Observations on the Perils (and Rewards) of Artmaking by David Bayles and Ted Orland

Bird by Bird: Some Instructions on Writing and Life by Anne Lamott

Letters to a Young Poet by Rainer Maria Rilke

A Portrait of the Artist as a Young Man by James Joyce

That's it. There are other brilliant books about creativity—from Sir Ken Robinson and Twyla Tharp and many more—but perhaps reading them only keeps us out of the doing. So make it a both/and equation. For every book on creativity you read, you must spend six months simply creating. Every single day.

If you'd like to post the index card art you create as you go through the "Give Yourself 10" and "Give Yourself 37" exercises in this book (and see what others are creating), go to www.pattidigh.com and look for the Creative Is a Verb tab.

Artists

Page x Leah Piken Kolidas, http://bluetreeartgallery/com; **page 4** Kim de Broin Mailhot, http://queen-of-arts.blogspot.com; **page 6** Kathy Iannucci; **page 12** Allyson McDuffie, http://allycatstudio.blogspot.com; **page 14** Ruth M. Davis; **page 16** Erica Hanson, http://writingisconversation.blogspot.com; **page 19** Linda C. Bannan; **page 22** Elizabeth Bailey, www.nfluxus.com; **page 24** Deneé Black; **page 26** Gwyn Michael, http://gwynmichael.com; **page 30** Kim de Broin Mailhot, www.queen-of-arts.blogspot.com; **page 32** Mary M. Meares; **page 33** Gwyn Michael, http://gwynmichael.com; **page 36** Tess Ptak; **page 37** Tony Stowers; **page 38** Tari Goerlitz, www.studiomailbox.com; **page 41** Kathryn Antyr, www.truenortharts.com; **page 42** Christine Martell, http://christinemartell.com; **page 43** Heidi Hooten; **page 44** Kathryn Antyr, www.truenortharts.com; **page 45** Elizabeth M. Reynolds, www.languageofthelens.blogspot.com; **page 46** Angélique J. Weger; **page 47** Cheryl Bakke Martin, www.inspirations-studio.com and http://inspirationsstudio.blogspot.com; **page 50** Ruth M. Davis; **page 52** Heather M. Muse; **page 54** Jessica Massey, www.jmasseydesign.com; **page 55** Lila Wells, www.BeingLila.blogspot.com; **page 57** Carolie DuBose Brekke, www.wordmagix.com; **page 62** Emma Ptak; **page 63** Davielle Huffman; **page 64** Kathy Iannucci; **page 67** Kate McGovern, www.katemcgovernphoto.com; **page 68** Wendy McGowen; **page 71** Debbie Overton, www.debbieoverton.com; **page 72** Brenda Z. Lux; **page 73** Tresha Barger, http://bakbay.wordpress.com; **page 74** Wendee Higa Lee; **page 77** Carol B. Sloan, www.carolbsloan.blogspot.com; **page 78** Sylvia Barnowski, http://fiftytwosteps.blogspot.com; **page 81** Kylie Dinning; **page 82** Edie Evans-Bisbee, http://hootenannyhollow.blogspot.com; **page 83** Dawn Meisch, www.dirtykitchen.com; **page 84** Andrea L. Stern, http://andibeads.blogspot.com; **page 85** Connie Dooley, http://its6am.blogspot.com; **page 86** Lynn Weekes Karegeannes; **page 87** Fiona Lucas, www.glassoffashion.com; **page 88** Tara Lynn Melton-Miller; **page 90** Laura Allen, www.hungryforlifeblog.com; **page 92** Linda C. Bannan; **page 93** Kim Roberts Meacham, www.kimrobertsmeacham.com; Marie Maynard Tyndall; **page 94** Gwyn Michael, http://gwynmichael.com; **page 95** Kathryn Ruth Schuth; **page 97** Paula J. Kelly; **page 98** Linda C. Bannan; **page 99** Marsha Gaspari; **page 101** Cindy Bock, www.ncbungalows.com; **page 102** Deb Harpster, http://lananadoula.com; **page 104** Sheryl Eggleston, http://sheryleggleston.blogspot.com; **page 105** Kim Candlish, http://thebodhichicklet.blogspot.com; **page 106** Paula Bogdan, http://littlescrapsofmagic.typepad.com; **page 107** Susan Kinne; **page 110** Shawn Borror, http://oceanlotus.blogspot.com; **page 111** Anne E. Christ, westothemoondesigns.com/moonlight; **page 114** Dana Loffland; **page 115** Janine King Slaatte; **page 117** Patricia Tinsman-Schaffer, www.absolutearts.com/portfolios/p/pattitinsman; **page 118** Nina Newton, www.mamaslittletreasures.typepad.com; **page 119** Teresa Hartley; **page 121** Monica Moran aka The Creative Beast can be found at www.thecreativebeast.blogspot.com; **page 122** Amy A. Crawley, http://amyacrawley.com; **page 124** Marsha Gaspari, Carmella Michals; **page 125** Carolie DuBose Brekke, www.wordmagix.com; **page 126** Janet A. Smith, http://janetasmith.blogspot.com; **page 127** Sarah Davis, Bristol, ME, USA; **page 128** Heather M. Muse; **page 129** Lisa K. Smith; **page 130** Mary Alice Coussoulos; **page 131** Kara Brown, www.karabrownlovesart.com; **page 133** Sherry Smyth, www.bellarennie.etsy.com; **page 134** T. J. Johnson, http://tinkerart.typepad.com; **page 135** Susan Nash, http://sewmuchart.blogspot.com; **page 137** Beverly Gwinn Jones, http://twocoyotesstudio.com; **page**

Permissions

Gratitudes

What deep and generous communities I belong to . . . To readers of my blog, 37days, a special note of thanks for joining me on the journey and enriching the way I see the world. To my friends on Twitter and Facebook, the creative tribes into which you've welcomed me belie the belief of some that online friendships aren't real. Indeed they are. A special thanks to Sven Cahling for a video I will never forget, of *Life Is a Verb* taking a bike ride across a small bridge in Sweden just after it was published.

With special thanks also to David Robinson who has taught me more deeply about creativity than anyone else I know. And to David and Jodi Cohen for late-night "what is essential?" sessions at the Bend of Ivy Lodge. My thanks also to neighbors Emma and Hilary Drake, and Pam Brown, for opening their homes to me and my friends.

With thanks to my high school art teacher, David Sheets, for being such an important creative influence early on. To Frank and Mary Ptak for their unending support and love. And to my mother, Frances Hardin, and *her* father, my granddaddy, L. E. Ramsey, whose hand-loomed pot holders were an early lesson about what it means to be creative.

With thanks to my "bros," Stuart Zitin and Tyrone Greenlee, for hearing me out once a month at our Clingman Café coffee conversations. To Dave Walens who unwittingly became a trusted adviser just by being assigned the seat next to mine on a plane trip from San Diego to Atlanta. Bless his heart. I think he really had planned to sleep on that flight. To Kathryn Ruth Schuth and Amy McCracken for being two of the most creative people I've ever known. To Howard Holden, of course, because I love him. Mushy alert, Howard. And to Nina McIntosh for the same reason and for all the lessons she is teaching me daily while making me laugh at the same time.

With deep appreciation to the artists and poets whose work graces this book as well as my past two books. They are the greatest example of what it means to live a fully creative life. And of generosity of spirit.

To my editor, Mary Norris, whose full-color photo is now featured in Wikipedia under both "Patience" and "Clarity."

In appreciation for the fact that my old cat Sim Sim still sits on my lap every time I write. May she be there for the next book as well.

And, finally, with thanks to John, Emma, and Tess Ptak, for teaching me simply everything (EVERYTHING) I know and love.

About the Author

© Michael Mauney

I am an optimist. I am proud to be naive. I love having great hope in a world that sometimes seems hopeless. I like to laugh. I write a thank-you note every morning. I am also quite fond of peonies and the smell of lavender. —**Patti Digh**

"If the Buddha had two kids, a dog named Blue, and a huge crush on Johnny Depp, his name would be Patti Digh," wrote one reviewer.

Whatever else she has done and seen and created in her life—circum-navigating the globe on a ship in charge of 600 teenagers, working in a batik factory in Sri Lanka as a teenager herself, eating lunch with novelist Carlos Fuentes, interviewing Stevie Wonder in her pajamas, traveling to more than sixty countries—Patti Digh is most importantly a mom.

Patti is the award-winning author of several business books that were creative in the way business books seldom are, and also of the grassroots best seller *Life Is a Verb: 37 Days to Wake Up, Be Mindful, and Live Intentionally,* which was a 2008 finalist for the prestigious "Books for a Better Life" award and a nominee for the Southern Independent Booksellers' Association "Book of the Year." Her blog, 37days.com, brings together readers from ages twelve through ninety-five across the globe. Patti speaks to audiences all over the world and lives in the beautiful mountain town of Asheville, North Carolina, with her brilliant husband, John Ptak, and their two interesting and curious daughters, Emma and Tess. Patti has a fondness for social justice, Ginger Chews, exclamation points, the word *wee,* children's artwork, kilts, porch sitting, Mr. Johnny Depp, and Airstream trailers.

Be in touch, OK?

Twitter: @pattidigh / Facebook: www.tinyurl.com/pattidighpage

Blog: www.37days.com / Web: www.pattidigh.com

E-mail: patti@pattidigh.com

Snail: Patti Digh, 37days, P.O. Box 18323, Asheville, NC 28814, USA